Frank Sutherland Davidson

BUSH DREAMING
AND OTHER PLAYS

BY
FRANK SUTHERLAND DAVIDSON

Edited by Tracy Rockwell

PEGASUS PUBLISHING

Frank Sutherland Davidson

Bush Dreaming: And Other Plays

First Published in Australia in 2020

by
Frank Sutherland Davidson (1934)
Edited by Tracy Rockwell

Orders: pegasuspublishing@iinet.net.au
www.pegasuspublishing.com.au

PO Box 980, Edgecliff, NSW, 2027

Copyright © Pegasus Publishing
An Ashnong Pty Ltd Company

All rights reserved. No part of this publication may be reproduced, stored in a retrieval system, or transmitted in any form or by any means, electronic, mechanical, photocopying, recording or otherwise, without the prior written permission of the copyright owner.

A CIP catalogue record for this book is available from the National Library of Australia.

ISBN: 978-1-925909-02-9

Printed on Demand by Ingram Lightning Source
www.ingramspark.com

Cover Image:
'Outback, Australia landscape nature waterhole,' by Samillemitchell [undated (pixabay.com) from Needpix.com. Available at "https://www.needpix.com/photo/download/570557/outback-australia-landscape-nature-waterhole-free-pictures-free-photos-free-images-royalty-free."

BUSH DREAMING
AND OTHER PLAYS

BY
FRANK SUTHERLAND DAVIDSON

Edited by Tracy Rockwell

PEGASUS PUBLISHING

Frank Davidson

Frank Sutherland Davidson graduated with Honours in Geography and later, a Doctorate in Australian Literature from the University of New England. He was the first President of New England University Dramatic Society (NEUDS) and acted in the University's entries in Inter-Varsity Drama Festivals in Sydney and Hobart. After teaching in High Schools he accepted a position at Wollongong Teachers' College, and later at Sydney Teachers' College, as Lecturer in English, Speech and Drama. To equip himself for this he undertook a year's study at London University, investigating 'Theatre-in-Education' work in English schools, for which he was awarded Associateship of the University's Institute of Education. Apart from a number of academic papers he is also the author of a lighthearted crime novel entitled "The Coral Airlines Mystery." [ISBN: 978-1-4931-0186-3].

CONTENTS

TEN-MINUTE PLAYS
A Match Made In Heaven... 15
The Second Cuppa... 20
An Author In Search Of A Climax... 30
Family Fugue... 36
Mrs Boardman Widens Her Horizons... 43
By The Sea Wall... 50
Trouble On Noah's Ark... 57
Marleen's Wedding... 64
One In The Bath... 71
Justin's First Assignment... 78

SKETCHES & MONOLOGUES
Jarrod & Pete... 88
The Morning After... 91
Lotto Logic... 94
Twenty Years After... 96
In The Mood For Music... 99
Saleyard Saga... 101
Cafe Encounter... 105
Coming Home Today... 109
Prison... 112

PLAYS FOR CHILD AUDIENCES
The Magician's Cloak... 119
Above The Sky & Beyond The Stars... 137
The Mystery Of The Black Moon... 157

LONGER ONE-ACT PLAYS
Telling Barbie... 185
Bush Dreaming 202

Frank Sutherland Davidson

PREFACE

Frank Davidson's collection of short plays, monologues and sketches is as broad in scope and content as our lives are in reality. From his monologues to his 10 minute plays to his longer one acts, Frank shows us what living means – the dramas, the sadness, the joys, the fun and the challenges. His writing traverses the poetic and dramatic to the realistic and comic. All the works are evocative and terrific material to be read or acted out.

Bush Dreaming is a play set ostensibly in the desert with a female media celebrity (the Woman) stranded as a result of her vehicle breaking down. However, it deftly moves to a surreal, dreamlike other world inhabited by the Brolga with knowledge we all yearn to know, but so seldom recognise. What the Woman learns as the play unfolds provides her with a new perspective on the superficial life she has lived. "Lost creatures find new pastures and the fish that live in the desert hatch out of the mud. The weak will find a new strength." Through a conversation with the mysterious Gavin (the Man), Bush Dreaming is an examination of what really counts in our living world, and asks the question whether there a more authentic and honest way that we might dream to live.

In the Magicians Cloak, one of three children's plays in this volume, Frank draws on all the tropes of the fairy tale to tell a tale of good versus evil with, of course, good winning out. It is full of adventure and spells with some catchy rhyming sections as the Magician, the good ruler of his kingdom, Zepherina the Magician's daughter and Prince Quentin, with the help of magical trees and a rock fairy, overcome Viperella a wicked witch. All three plays are perfect material for use by primary/ infant teachers as well as parents . The plays can be acted out by children or can be equally read as the words evoke an imaginary word that will entice the interest of the young.

The Ten-Minute Plays are snippets of life as it passes us by. Frank has written them caringly with his unique and occasionally oblique insight into the human condition. They can be stark and confronting (A Match Made in Heaven), expose the vicissitudes of love in relationships (The Second Cuppa, Author In Search Of A Climax), are theatrically fun (Author In Search Of A Climax), play with class, money and sexuality (Mrs Boardman Widens Her Horizons), explore the possibility of suicide (By The Sea Wall), amuse us with a blind date gone wrong (One In The Bath), and fantasise about Hitler and Churchill surviving the war (Justin's First Assignment). Some make us laugh and some make us think anew. All provide rich material for actors to explore.

Sketches and Monologues are set in worlds and situations we easily recognise. They begin something that the reader or audience can imagine further or leave hanging. They touch lightly and often surprisingly on relationships on the cusp of something to be realised or unrealised, generosity unleashed, old schools friends, sexuality revealed, social gossip and snobbery, infidelity and violence and the loneliness of prison-life.

This volume of 'Bush Dreaming And Other Plays' is as entertaining as it is revealing of the human condition. It will serve well anyone interested in the power of plays and language to reveal the many facets of our society and the diverse and unique characters that inhabit it.

Robert Love
Riverside Theatres, Parramatta
September 2020

Frank Sutherland Davidson

FOREWORD

I first met Frank at Sydney Teachers' College where we worked together on many courses. The collaboration continued when the College became part of Sydney University. Over time this association developed into a friendship, which has continued into retirement.

His close observation of human nature and his fine sense of the ridiculous, which were always apparent, have stood him in good stead for his drama teaching and his writing. I have been privileged to watch him in drama activities with students ranging in age from six years old to middle age. He has also mentored me in my work with students of all ages. Much of this activity later grew into more formal scripts, which I notice are included in this volume, particularly in the plays for children.

After retirement I had the privilege of watching a number of Frank's plays performed in the Short and Sweet Festival. I remember "The Second Cuppa" particularly and was delighted to be there when it's cast won the best actor, and runner up for best actress awards at the festival. I regret I have not seen many more of his plays performed, but nonetheless can enjoy the scripts.

I am very pleased to see all this work assembled in one volume and am sure you will enjoy it as much as I have.

Ms. Kerry Cameron *(M.A.(Hons); Dip. Ed.)*

INTRODUCTION

This collection reflects an interest I have had since childhood in the wonderful way that drama, especially as seen in the theatre, can illuminate life.

Having mentioned childhood, being born in the country I grew up virtually without playmates, but I do remember at about the age of six trying to remedy the deficiency by directing the farm's pet lambs in various stories that I tried to enact with them. Professional theatre people might sympathise with the fact that these independent creatures very seldom obeyed my instructions and would take off in all directions, pursued by a frustrated director.

For me, theatre has always been a hobby rather than a profession, although as Section 3 of this book illustrates, I did at one stage have the responsibility of teaching it. And, of course, as life progressed I have taken part as an actor in a number of amateur and semi-professional theatre groups, such as the company at The Australian Theatre, Newtown, founded and administered by the late Dr Amy McGrath.

I hope that anyone purchasing this book will feel free to make use of its contents, some items of which I have been fortunate enough to see performed, and many of which can be used as exercises in the performing arts and programme fillers.

Frank S. Davidson

Frank Sutherland Davidson

TEN MINUTE PLAYS

The world-wide phenomenon of the Crash Test Drama 10-minute play contests, made popular in Australia, the USA and elsewhere by playwright Alex Broun (www.alex.broun.com) has resulted in many writers trying their luck with this specialised format. Some of the following scripts have been entered in Crash Test performances in Sydney... with acclaim.

However, most have been tried out by another valuable group of writers, actors and directors... many people doubling or tripling these roles. This group, containing both professional and fringe theatre people in a happy mixture of both, is Script in Hand, a voluntary organisation which meets monthly in Sydney to try out new writing for the theatre.

I am grateful to all actors and directors who have had a hand in trying out most of the following scripts and presenting them in rehearsed readings.

Frank Sutherland Davidson

A MATCH MADE IN HEAVEN

Is death the end, or can it be the beginning?

Cast: MOSHE, a male Israeli soldier,
IDRIS, a Palestinian female suicide bomber.

Setting: *Limbo. It is dimly lit but a bit of mist swirls around. Spots come up L and R as appropriate. MOSHE enters L, bloodstained and tattered etc.*

MOSHE: Oy vey. It's dark in here. Where's the field ambulance? Where's my oxygen mask? Oh my god. I've lost my rifle *(feels himself all over)* And my grenades! What's happened to my grenades? Don't panic Moshe. Remember, God is with you. God is on your side *(yells)* God! My grenades! You didn't take 'em, did you God?? *(pause)* Don't leave me unprotected like this!! *(crouches down in a protective position)*

(IDRIS enters R. She is also bloodstained and her clothes are in tatters).

IDRIS: Praise be to Allah. It is done. Now, at last, I am happy. And it is true... I feel no pain. Oh... I am a Martyr! Allah be praised, I have redeemed my family name.

MOSHE: That girl. I've seen her before. When she looked at me, my heart turned over *(to IDRIS)* Hoy! You were in the market. My platoon cordoned it off. But you wouldn't go *(gesticulates)* Go on! Go on! Get out of here! It isn't safe here.

IDRIS: It is very safe. I am on my way to Paradise. I am treading in the footsteps of all the Martyrs who have gone before.

MOSHE: *(Not understanding)* What?

IDRIS: I have fulfilled my destiny. I have justified the faith of my leader.

MOSHE: You should be dead.

IDRIS: (*Laughing*) I am dead.

MOSHE: That bomb... that bomber... it wasn't you, was it?

IDRIS: Allah is great.

MOSHE: Dead? You mean...

IDRIS: We are both dead, soldier. You're not very bright, are you.

MOSHE: I just follow orders. I was supposed to clear the area of civilians...

IDRIS: But I had a divine purpose, and I stayed.

MOSHE: So... it was you let off the bomb! You're a suicide bomber.

IDRIS: That is not correct. With Allah's help I have fulfilled a successful mission in the holy intifadeh. It is done. I go towards my reward.

MOSHE: You... you shouldn't have died...

IDRIS: Your mind is slow (*teasing*) You must be a very poor soldier (*with some bitterness*) Perhaps you are no better than all the other invaders who would take our land away from us, divide our families and punish our innocent children.

MOSHE: You mean... (*gasps*) I must be dead too?

IDRIS: You find it difficult to accept the reality, don't you.

MOSHE: (*In disbelief*) Dead.

IDRIS: Finally you begin to understand. You know... you remind me of my little brother. He too is very slow to understand. But you... you are a soldier. You should know that death can come at any time. Especially in war.

MOSHE: It's not what I expected.

IDRIS: That is the difference between us. When I gave my life to God I knew exactly what to expect. But you. You give your God nothing. What does your god expect of you? That you come into our country, and

	murder us all with your American weapons, your tanks and your mortars...
MOSHE:	It's a war. I do my duty.
IDRIS:	Your duty is nothing. It is the sand before the wind, that has shifted with each rising of the sun.
MOSHE:	You really are that bomber, aren't you. I saw you... you had a backpack...
IDRIS:	Yes, I am "that bomber".
MOSHE:	And you're proud of it.
IDRIS:	Yes. I am proud.
MOSHE:	Proud to murder?
IDRIS:	Proud to avenge the death of my father.
MOSHE:	So you kill fifty to avenge one?
IDRIS:	The numbers are immaterial. My father is avenged.
MOSHE:	(*As though finally realising it*) And me. You've killed... me.
IDRIS:	Yes; it is so.
MOSHE:	But in the market. When I saw you. I looked into your eyes, and I saw peace.
IDRIS:	Yes. I saw that look of yours. That look in your eyes. And I moved towards it.
MOSHE:	To take my life from me.
IDRIS:	No. To give myself to you, in death.
MOSHE:	You're... that's... it's...
IDRIS:	(*Going to him*) Unless you have words to say, do not speak.
MOSHE:	I would have loved you.
IDRIS:	You do love me. I saw it, in the market, the instant our eyes met.
MOSHE:	And yet...
IDRIS:	Yes. I killed us both.

MOSHE: And yet...

IDRIS: And yet I love you still.

MOSHE: I didn't want death! I wanted life. I wanted to bring honour to my father and mother, to keep the Commandments, to have children of my own, a wife to love.

IDRIS: But it is too late. In the world we have left, our love itself was death.

MOSHE: And what is this world. This world you have sent me to, that I don't understand.

IDRIS: (*Inspired*) The world that I have brought you to. The journey we will take together. To the gates of Paradise.

MOSHE: (*Peering around*) You mean... this is the holy Cave?

IDRIS: The cave?

MOSHE: You wouldn't understand. You are not one of the chosen.

IDRIS: You are wrong, soldier. My name is Idris el Bakhtir and today I join the Martyrs in Paradise.

MOSHE: You're in the wrong place. If we're really dead this has got to be the Cave that leads to the door to the Garden of Eden, and soon the blinding light of the Patriarchs will shine and you will be pushed into the wilderness.

IDRIS: (*Laughing*) Oh no. You really believe that.

MOSHE: It is what we are taught.

IDRIS: You are taught wrongly.

MOSHE: Oh. And I suppose you think that all that claptrap about Paradise is really going to happen.

IDRIS: If I believe, it is true. That is all.

MOSHE: All that seventy virgins stuff.

IDRIS: Allah is great (*sounds of a mighty wind, growing in intensity as dialogue continues*).

MOSHE: Well you're right about one thing. We're never going back.

IDRIS: No *(they begin slow motion moves L and R in the opposite direction to their entrances)*.

MOSHE: I can feel it. The Light is shining.

IDRIS: I hear the music of the fountains.

MOSHE: The door is opening.

IDRIS: I see the open arms of the Martyrs.

MOSHE: The Patriarchs are beckoning me

IDRIS & MOSHE: *(Together)* I will live forever... today I enter Paradise, *(they half-turn, to semi-face each other again)*... I will love you forever.

IDRIS: Till the winds take the sands from the desert.

MOSHE: Till the rocks melt in the sun.

IDRIS: Goodbye... my love.

MOSHE: My love that never was... goodbye *(they have gone)*.

Frank Sutherland Davidson

THE SECOND CUPPA

Trouble getting a second cup of tea at breakfast time.

Cast:	HARVEY, *a middle-aged Australian male,* IRENE, *his wife.*

Setting: *A breakfast table. HARVEY and IRENE are seated having breakfast. HARVEY is reading the newspaper.*

HARVEY: *(Holding out his cup)* Just give me another cuppa tea, willya love?

IRENE: No; I won't.

HARVEY: What!?

IRENE: No, I won't give you another cuppa tea. You can just get up and get it yourself.

HARVEY: Aw, cripes, what's a man done now.

IRENE: You don't know, don't expect me to tell you.

HARVEY: You mean I gotta guess.

IRENE: *(Shrugs)* Up to you.

HARVEY: So, what I done, whatever it is, it's so bad, I gotta get me own cuppa.

IRENE: You got it in one.

HARVEY: Well, you've got the teapot there. Right in front of you.

IRENE: Don't expect me to pass it.

HARVEY: Oh no... too heavy, I bet.

IRENE: A man aught to have more sensitivity.

HARVEY: Sensy what?

IRENE: Sensitivity. You wouldn't know.

HARVEY: If I wouldn't know, how can I have it?

IRENE: Should come natural.

HARVEY:	That's more like it. I noticed you didn't object last night, when I came natural.
IRENE:	Ooh, don't speak to me.
HARVEY:	In the nude, too, you was.
IRENE:	You aught to be ashamed.
HARVEY:	What of?
IRENE:	You don't know how a woman feels.
HARVEY:	Yes, I do. Feels great.
IRENE:	That's not what I meant.
HARVEY:	Well, how do I know what you meant, if you don't tell me?
IRENE:	You should know without me telling you.
HARVEY:	(*Mimicking*) You should know without me telling you.
IRENE:	Well, you should.
HARVEY:	Well, I don't.
IRENE:	Well, it's time you found out.
HARVEY:	Great. So I gotta find out without even gettin' me second cuppa tea.
IRENE:	I don't care how you find out, I'm not passing you the teapot and that's flat.
HARVEY:	(*Gets up, walks away from table during following dialogue*) Well, I might have to have a beer instead.
IRENE:	You would.
HARVEY:	Yeah, if I can't have a cuppa tea, have to do the next best thing.
IRENE:	Next best thing? Don't make me laugh.
HARVEY:	I didn't notice you was laughing.
IRENE:	I wasn't.
HARVEY:	You told me you was.
IRENE:	No I didn't. What I said was, I wasn't going to laugh.

HARVEY: Well why would you. I haven't noticed anything funny.

IRENE: Except you.

HARVEY: Me? Why?

IRENE: The idea... (*chuckles dryly*).

HARVEY: What idea?

IRENE: That you'd prefer a cuppa tea instead of a beer.

HARVEY: Well, I'm not gettin' a cuppa tea, by the looks of it, so I might have to settle for a beer. That's what I said... (*sits down again*).

IRENE: You drink too much.

HARVEY: What a thing to say. I've only had one cuppa this morning. So far.

IRENE: I didn't mean tea. I meant beer.

HARVEY: How would you know?

IRENE: Well, you had too much last night, that's for sure.

HARVEY: Didn't affect me prowess, did it?

IRENE: Ooh, don't talk to me.

HARVEY: Why're you all clammed up this morning? You was very talkative, last night, you was.

IRENE: I wasn't drunk. Not like you.

HARVEY: You reckon I was drunk last night? (*laughs*) You shoulda seen me after the footie last week.

IRENE: I did.

HARVEY: Funny, I didn't notice you at the footie.

IRENE: I wasn't there. I just tried not to notice you, when you got home.

HARVEY: Yeah, I tried not to make too much noise.

IRENE: Didn't seem to work, did it.

HARVEY: Whaddya mean?

IRENE: Blind as a bat, you were.

HARVEY:	Well, I couldn't find the light switch.
IRENE:	Wouldn't have made any difference, if you had. You were still as blind as a bat.
HARVEY:	Anyway. Why didn't you leave the light on? Might've been able to see where I was going.
IRENE:	I always turn it off when I go to bed.
HARVEY:	Well, you went to bed too early.
IRENE:	No I didn't. It was nine o'clock.
HARVEY:	That late, was it.
IRENE:	And the footie finished at five.
HARVEY:	Yeah, went on with some of the blokes and had a beer at the Olympic.
IRENE:	Had a beer! What a joke. You were loaded. You must have had about thirteen.
HARVEY:	Who's counting?
IRENE:	Well, you obviously weren't.
HARVEY:	Why would I count beers while I'm having them?
IRENE:	Funny that it seems to be different when it comes to tea. You seem to know exactly how many cups of tea you've had this morning.
HARVEY:	Yeah, just the one... so far.
IRENE:	And don't think I'm going to pass you the teapot.
HARVEY:	Probably cold by now, anyway... (*he takes up the newspaper again*).
IRENE:	The point is, you should know more about how I feel about things.
HARVEY:	What things?
IRENE:	Well, you know.
HARVEY:	Wish I did.
IRENE:	Like last night, for instance.
HARVEY:	Last night? What was wrong with last night?

IRENE: It's just that...

HARVEY: What?

IRENE: Well, this morning, you seem to have forgotten all about it.

HARVEY: No I haven't. It was a bloody beauty.

IRENE: Yes, well; how would I know?

HARVEY: I told ya. It was great. Better than anything.

IRENE: Even the booze?

HARVEY: Hey, go on. What's all this about?

IRENE: Sometimes I feel that you don't like... well, you know, unless you're tanked up.

HARVEY: Don't be stupid.

IRENE: Oh, great. That's what I don't like about you. You've got no sensitivity.

HARVEY: (*Throws down newspaper*) Yeah, I better get going. Got to find out where to get it. Whatever it is.

IRENE: It means, thinking about the other person, sometimes.

HARVEY: You reckon I wasn't thinking about you? While we was doin' the horizontal tango? Give me a break.

IRENE: Well how would I know. You never say anything.

HARVEY: Too busy, usually.

IRENE: That's just it. It's all over and you just go away.

HARVEY: What're you talking about? I would've had trouble standin' up, after givin' me all (*mutters*) Couldn't hardly get to the bathroom afterwards.

IRENE: I don't mean go away.

HARVEY: You just said go away. I was there all night. You even complained this morning about me snoring.

IRENE: You always do, when you've had too much.

HARVEY: Here we go again.

IRENE:	It's not just when you're drunk.
HARVEY:	I wasn't drunk. Not last night.
IRENE:	Not as drunk, maybe.
HARVEY:	Not as drunk as what?
IRENE:	As usual.
HARVEY:	Cripes! I only ever really get on the piss when I go to the footie.
IRENE:	Or when Joe comes round, or Andy, or Mick...
HARVEY:	Well, you've gotta be hospitable.
IRENE:	I don't.
HARVEY:	Aw, give us a break.
IRENE:	Look. There are some things a woman needs to know.
HARVEY:	Like what?
IRENE:	I've been trying to tell you.
HARVEY:	Been a bit obscure.
IRENE:	Maybe to somebody with a head as thick as two planks.
HARVEY:	Glad you don't mean me.
IRENE:	Yes I do.
HARVEY:	Two planks?
IRENE:	Don't you try to change the subject.
HARVEY:	Oh no. Great to have a chat about hardware for a change. What is your opinion about the magnetic carpentry clamp?
IRENE:	The what?
HARVEY:	Doesn't matter.
IRENE:	If you must know, a woman needs to feel... wanted.
HARVEY:	Wanted! You're bloody essential.
IRENE:	It would be nice if you told me that sometimes.

HARVEY: I just did! Bloody hell.

IRENE: I mean, without being reminded.

HARVEY: (*Leans back, toys with a newspaper*) Well, you know how I forget things. I do get a bit forgetful sometimes. Like when you make me go and do the shopping.

IRENE: I haven't asked you to do any shopping for years. I wouldn't risk it. Last time you did, you came home with a Black & Decker drill instead of the sausages.

HARVEY: Yeah, went to Bunnings instead of the butcher's.

IRENE: Funny kind of mistake to make.

HARVEY: Well, they're right next door to each other.

IRENE: That's what I mean. You don't notice.

HARVEY: Anything I don't notice isn't important.

IRENE: Oh, wonderful. I suppose that means I'm not important.

HARVEY: Who says I don't notice you?

IRENE: I do. I just did.

HARVEY: Look. Just tell me what I have to say to get another cuppa tea, and I'll say it. No sweat.

IRENE: Typical. I have to tell you everything.

HARVEY: That's if you want me to know.

IRENE: It would be good if just once you could work it out for yourself.

HARVEY: You know what they say. "A problem shared is a problem squared".

IRENE: You can't even get that right. It's "a problem shared is a problem halved."

HARVEY: Well, it's probably the same thing.

IRENE: It obviously is, to you, but that doesn't mean it is.

HARVEY: Look. I know what you're doin'. You're holdin' out on me because I haven't said something you want me to say. Right?

IRENE: Yes.
HARVEY: OK, I'll say it.
IRENE: Go ahead... (*pause*).
HARVEY: What is it?
IRENE: I'd just like you to tell me... when you... you know... that I'm still... attractive.
HARVEY: Jeez, with a few beers in, anybody'd be attractive... I mean...
IRENE: That's it. You're hopeless. You drink too much. You're a male chauvinist or whatever they call them. Pig. You're a male chauvinist pig. You know... p.i.g. (*she snorts, like a pig, to emphasise the point*).
HARVEY: Cripes, that was sudden.
IRENE: Sudden! It's been coming on for years.
HARVEY: You might of warned me.
IRENE: Warned you! You wouldn't notice if the Harbour Bridge fell on you.
HARVEY: (*Serious*) That's a real stupid thing to say. I wouldn't be underneath the bloody Harbour Bridge.
IRENE: No. You'd be too busy with your snout in the trough at the Olympic.
HARVEY: What's wrong with the Olympic? It's a real good pub.
IRENE: Good for pigs.
HARVEY: Oh, give over.
IRENE: So the only thing left for me to think, is that you don't love me anymore.
HARVEY: What? Why would you think a thing like that?
IRENE: You never say.
HARVEY: Well, you already know.
IRENE: Yes, but I'd like to be reassured sometimes. Like last night.

HARVEY: Well, that was last night.

IRENE: So you don't feel the same this morning. You thought you loved me last night, but you've changed your mind this morning, is that it.

HARVEY: No, it's not bloody it.

IRENE: What's wrong with speaking what's on your mind?

HARVEY: You really want to know what's on my mind? Are you sure?

IRENE: Yes. I want to know.

HARVEY: Well then. I think you're the most bloody cantankerous woman that I've ever known, I think you never give a man a moment's peace, and I think you'd drive a bloody Methodist to drink (*rattles his empty cup*) As long as it wasn't tea he was after.

IRENE: You mean that?

HARVEY: Of course. Would I say it if I didn't mean it?

IRENE: So. Now we know where we are then.

HARVEY: Oh, and I forgot to say. I love you; real bad.

IRENE: You what?

HARVEY: I said, I love you. Real bad, I said.

IRENE: (*She has melted*) Even though I drive you to drink?

HARVEY: Thought you'd never offer (*holding out his cup*) What about a second cuppa?

IRENE: Not yet.

HARVEY: Don't bloody tell me you want me to say more than what I've bloody said all bloody ready.

IRENE: No; I think you've done as well as any male chauvinist pig could be expected to do.

HARVEY: What then?

IRENE: (*She rises*) Well, I'll just go and put the jug on, and hot up the teapot (*she makes to exit*) I wouldn't want you to have to tell people that I gave you a cold cuppa tea for breakfast.

	(IRENE EXITS.)
HARVEY:	Hey. D'you want a hand?
IRENE:	(*Very coyly*) I wouldn't mind.
	(HARVEY EXITS in a hurry).

Frank Sutherland Davidson

AN AUTHOR IN SEARCH OF A CLIMAX

Who said creating a masterpiece was easy?

Cast: DAMIEN, a writer,
LEWIS }
SPIRO }
CONNIE } all actors in rehearsal.
ANGIE }

Setting: Lights come up on the following scene: A bare room, with two double-seated sofas L and R and an armchair C. There is a potted palm on a stand next to the chair.
Blackout... (pause)... A shot is heard... (pause)... CONNIE screams. Lights come on to discover a seated group of five. DAMIEN, slumped in the armchair C, a bloodstained chest, apparently dead. The others in pairs L and R.

CONNIE: My god!

LEWIS: Where's the gun?

SPIRO: Don't look at me.

ANGIE: Damien!

SPIRO: Gawd! I think he's...

LEWIS: Oh trust him. Just when things aren't going his way he goes and shoots himself.

CONNIE: Isn't anybody going to...

SPIRO: Don't look at me.

ANGIE: How can you be so heartless!

LEWIS: Well – go on! You go and feel his pulse.

ANGIE: (*Shrinking*) No! I've... I've never seen a dead body before.

LEWIS: Where's the gun?

CONNIE: Why doesn't somebody...

SPIRO: What's the point. He's dead.

ANGIE:	Yes but how...
LEWIS:	It's typical of Damien. He shoots himself and leaves us to carry the can.
CONNIE:	Is there a phone here?
ANGIE:	An ambulance! Call an ambulance!
LEWIS:	What good is an ambulance going to be!
CONNIE:	We have to do something!
SPIRO:	*(Laughs)* I reckon he's the one that should do something.
CONNIE:	Don't be silly. This is real. It's not a joke... is it?
LEWIS:	It's been a joke from the moment we came here.
ANGIE:	We can't all just stand here...
SPIRO:	Why not! It makes as much sense as all that rubbish he was going on with... before the lights went out.
CONNIE:	It was my cue.
ANGIE:	I didn't expect a real blackout.
LEWIS:	Look. If we don't do anything, things are going to get serious. We should call the police.
SPIRO:	And land us all up shit street without a paddle. I reckon we should find the gun first.
LEWIS:	How do we know you haven't got it, Spiro? You're the one who told him his dialogue was utter crap.
SPIRO:	So it is, but that's not a reason to shoot him.
LEWIS:	I reckon, when the police come, they'll probably want to search us.
SPIRO:	They won't find anything on me.
LEWIS:	So what did you do with the gun then, Spiro? Under the sofa is it? Down the pot plant? I hope you didn't forget to wipe your fingerprints off it.
ANGIE:	Oh stop, stop! If you don't stop bickering I'm going to have hysterics.

SPIRO: Oh poor widdle Angie-pangie. Go on, Angie, have your hysterics, Anything to relieve the boredom.

CONNIE: You really are a shit, aren't you Spiro.

SPIRO: Yes.

ANGIE: (*Wailing*) I liked him. I really did.

LEWIS: Don't give us that bullshit. None of us liked him...

SPIRO: Self-indulgent prick.

CONNIE: You can't go round eliminating people you don't like.

SPIRO: Yeah. Wouldn't be many left around here.

ANGIE: He didn't deserve to be shot...

SPIRO: Yes he did.

LEWIS: Poisoning's too slow.

CONNIE: You're both disgusting.

SPIRO: It's a bit of a laugh really (*he laughs*).

ANGIE: You're a... a sadist, Spiro. You really are.

LEWIS: Angie, I think the word you want is psychopathetic.

ANGIE: He shouldn't talk about Damien like that.

SPIRO: Oh ho! Had a bit of a thing for him did you Angie?

ANGIE: You are truly hateful Spiro.

SPIRO: Yes but accurate.

LEWIS: Ah! An accurate shot in the dark, are you, Spiro?

SPIRO: Oh lay off me. I heard what you said about him you know.

LEWIS: You heard nothing.

CONNIE: As a matter of fact... I heard you too. You said, that Damien would be better off dead than trying to write a play.

LEWIS: I said that? You must be joking.

CONNIE: That's what I heard.

LEWIS:	Bullshit.
CONNIE:	I heard it while you were doing your stupid warm-up.
LEWIS:	Typical of you. You're not even a real professional.
ANGIE:	I'm going to ring an ambulance *(gets mobile out of handbag)*.
LEWIS:	Oh for pete's sake. Why don't you ring the ABC while you're at it.
SPIRO:	Or the Alan Jones Program on ABC Radio.
CONNIE:	Getting worried are we boys? How do Angie and I know that you two didn't plan this together?
LEWIS:	Wouldn't waste my time.
CONNIE:	Oh! Too many professional engagements, perhaps.
SPIRO:	I wouldn't risk doing anything with him.
ANGIE:	My battery must be flat.
SPIRO:	A bit like your chest.
ANGIE:	*(In tears)* I hate you.
CONNIE:	This has gone far enough. I'm ringing the police. The longer we leave it the worse it'll get. *(She gets her mobile out of her handbag)*
SPIRO:	Don't tell me, yours'll be flat too.
CONNIE:	I can't get a line.
LEWIS:	Well that's that. We'll just have to wait for the cleaners.
CONNIE:	What sort of an idiot do you take me for? To sit around here, with Damien dead in his chair, until the cleaners come in and find him? You should be on "Home and Away".
LEWIS:	It has obviously escaped your notice. I have been on "Home and Away".
SPIRO:	For ten seconds, and that was cut.
LEWIS:	They paid me.

SPIRO: On the condition you never came back.

LEWIS: Oh very clever. Remind me never to introduce you to my agent.

ANGIE: Do you think we could break for a cup of tea? I'm exhausted.

SPIRO: Typical. You'd never last in a reality show.

CONNIE: If there was an electric kettle here I'd put it on.

(DAMIEN sits up impatiently, removes what has turned out to be a bloodstained handkerchief from his chest. Various reactions).

DAMIEN: Oh my god. That's enough! It's more than enough. It was absolutely ghastly. What I wanted you all to do was to sink your individuality and embrace the opportunity to take the situation I've created for you through to the next level. But instead – all you did was revert to your own personality types and wallow about in irrelevant clichés. What I want is actors... not self-opinionated little nonentities.

LEWIS: Who are you calling a nonentity.

DAMIEN: You, darling. Especially, you. *(To SPIRO)* And as for you... they don't come more unoriginal than what you served up... that old cliché of the romantic lead falling for the author... hopeless.

ANGIE: *(Muffled sob)*

SPIRO: Yes well at least I'm not a dead shit, like you.

DAMIEN: Not one of you rose to the occasion.

CONNIE: If only there'd been an occasion to rise to.

ANGIE: *(Inspired)* I've had an idea.

SPIRO: Not again. The heavens might fall.

ANGIE: Why don't we do it again?

DAMIEN: At last – a constructive suggestion. Positions everybody and I'll do the blackout.

CONNIE: That's sure to throw light on everything.

DAMIEN: Ready, everybody. And this time, I want vibrance, drama, tension, invention, verisimilitude, flowing dialogue, and climax, Climax, CLIMAX!

ANGIE: Ooh, goodie!

THE OTHERS: *(Variously)* Oh shit. More crap. What a wanker. Bullshit artist. etc etc.

ALL: *(Including DAMIEN, who remains alive, resume their original positions).*

Blackout... (pause)... A shot is heard... (pause)... Confused Voices. Lights up to discover DAMIEN dead in chair while CONNIE, LEWIS, ANGIE and SPIRO line up and start taking individual curtain calls. SPIRO may produce a gun and pass it along the row. Suitable music wells up.

As they exit, DAMIEN may revive, assess the situation and floridly take his own curtain call using his bloody handkerchief.

Frank Sutherland Davidson

FAMILY FUGUE

Where is love hiding?

Cast: AMANDA, *a 16 year old girl,*
BUSTER, *20 year old boyfriend of Amanda,*
CHERYL, *Amanda's mother, early 30's,*
BRAD, *Cheryl's boyfriend, aged 40 or so.*

Setting: *The stage is divided by lighting into two areas... AREA 1 (stage L) is Cheryl's living room; AREA 2 (stage R) is Brad's bedroom. Couch (L), double bed (R).*

The living room of Cheryl's flat. Enter AMANDA and BUSTER.

BUSTER: Don't you think it's a bit... too soon? To tell your mother we're together?

AMANDA: Why would it be too soon? We're gonna live together, aren't we? Next week we're gonna get our own flat. Miles away from here. She's gotta know sometime.

BUSTER: So you think she's gonna object, do you.

AMANDA: She usually objects... to everything.

BUSTER: Everything?

AMANDA: Yeah. I can't do anything right... it seems.

BUSTER: Well then, why would she think it's OK? I mean, you and me?

AMANDA: Look. I just don't care whether she does or not. I just want her to know that for once in my life I've made a decision that she hasn't forced on me.

BUSTER: So she's pretty rigid, huh.

AMANDA: You could say that. And it's not even that she's that old. I mean she had me when she was sixteen, for god's sake.

BUSTER: Same age as you are now.

AMANDA:	Yeah. Same age. I could be her. Only, I've got more sense than to get knocked up and have a kid trailing round after me.
BUSTER:	You can't blame her. I mean, for having you.
AMANDA:	It's not that. It's the way she always spoils everything. But it'll be different when I'm living with you. And, I'll have a job. That job you got me at the call centre? She won't be able to touch me, then. And we're gonna have the best time... you and me. Aren't we.
BUSTER:	Sure... (*they embrace and kiss*) Hey. What's she called?
AMANDA:	(*Shrugs*) Cheryl, I guess. That's what her boyfriend calls her. The one she's got now that is.
BUSTER:	She's got a permanent guy?
AMANDA:	Yeah. At the moment. Well I wouldn't say permanent. She changes them... pretty regular.
BUSTER:	What, like, one after another.
AMANDA:	Oh, some of 'em last a coupla months... then it's 'no way Hosea' time and before you know it she's got a different one in tow.
BUSTER:	Do they all come here?
AMANDA:	Some do. Man, some of 'em are real slobs too.
BUSTER:	Did any of 'em ever try it on with you?
AMANDA:	Has been known. This one did. The one she's got now.
BUSTER:	What did you do?
AMANDA:	(*Laughs*) Kicked him in the balls. Then I left. He wasn't here when I came back.
BUSTER:	Did he ever come back?
AMANDA:	Nah. She goes to his place now.
BUSTER:	So how long's she been going with him?
AMANDA:	Must be three weeks now, or a month, nearly.
BUSTER:	So... she doesn't really have a really permanent guy,

	then.
AMANDA:	Yeah. It's funny... it's like she's looking for something, and she can't find it.
BUSTER:	You mean... like she wants something different. Maybe, like, something different from each guy?
AMANDA:	Maybe. Or, maybe, she can't find anyone that can give her what she really wants. Not like me. I found you, and you're all I ever want. Ever.
BUSTER:	Hey. C'm here *(They embrace and kiss again).*
	(Lights fade on area 1... then lights come up on area 2).
Setting:	*Brad's bedroom. BRAD and CHERYL are in bed. She is frantically putting on her clothes.*
BRAD:	Hey, Cheryl. Babe. Don't go yet.
CHERYL:	Brad, I've got to. Amanda will be home by now.
BRAD:	Don't tell me the little bitch can't spend a bit of time on her own.
CHERYL:	You don't understand. I don't want her mooning around with nothing to do.
BRAD:	What do you expect her to do?
CHERYL:	I expect her to keep herself out of trouble, and unless I'm there I can't be sure what she'll get up to.
BRAD:	What's she likely to get up to, for Christ's sake.
CHERYL:	She's just at that age... when... if she's not careful...
BRAD:	You mean she might get involved with some big bad wolf. Get over it, Cheryl.
CHERYL:	It's all very well for you. You're not responsible. Amanda's my daughter. You wouldn't know.
BRAD:	*(With menacing gesture)* What that little smart-arse needs, is a good clip over the ear. If you had any sense at all that's what you'd do.
CHERYL:	I just don't know what made her so angry with you that day. She's so difficult.
BRAD:	I tell you, if she ever comes at me again, she'll get a

	boot right up the backside. No second chance.
CHERYL:	Don't you dare lay a finger on her.
BRAD:	I'll tell you what. I won't be round at your place again until you sort that little bitch out once and for all.
CHERYL:	Don't tell me what to do. With my own daughter.
BRAD:	Come back to bed.
CHERYL:	No. I'm going.
BRAD:	Suit yourself.
	(Lights down on area 2 and up on area 1...perhaps AMANDA and BUSTER are having sex. They climax with appropriate sounds as lights come up... AMANDA'S mobile rings).
AMANDA:	Oh god. It's her.
BUSTER:	Well aren't you going to answer it?
AMANDA:	*(Hesitates, then into the phone)* Hello? I'm at home *(pause)* What do you mean, is someone here? *(pause)* Well what if I did have someone here... *(pause)* I didn't say I had someone here. *(pause... she looks at Buster, who nods 'yes you do')* No. I'm on my own. I'm waiting for you to get home. All right, don't then. Stay there with him. Good bye.
BUSTER:	Why didn't you tell her? That I'm here? You'll never get anywhere with her if you lie to her.
AMANDA:	Whatever I say she won't believe me. So what's the point?
BUSTER:	You've got to start somewhere.
AMANDA:	It won't be today. Anyway, she's not coming home.
BUSTER:	How do you know?
AMANDA:	I can tell. I know her. She's rung from her boyfriend's place. That sleaze Brad. She'll be there for the duration. Now she thinks I'm here by myself.
BUSTER:	You mean... we've got the place to ourselves after all?

AMANDA: Seems like it.

BUSTER: Hey... c'm here *(they embrace)*.

(The lights fade on area 1... then lights come up on area 2... CHERYL returns and straddles BRAD on the bed.)

BRAD: So... you've decided to stay after all

CHERYL: Well... now that I know she's at home... I was just worried she might be seeing somebody.

BRAD: What if she was.

CHERYL: She's too young. It's so easy to go wrong, if you don't know. I don't want her making the same mistake I did.

BRAD: Get over it Cheryl. Any mistake she makes, it's her mistake, not yours. And talking of mistakes... you weren't thinking of leaving, now, were you? Because, you know, that really would be a very big, big, big, mistake.

CHERYL: I guess it's all right to stay... for a while. Oh Brad... I want you so much...

(They simulate intercourse as lights fade on area 2... then lights come up on area 1. BUSTER and AMANDA are lying side by side on the couch).

BUSTER: You know... I don't know what it is about you. But I just seem to want more and more of you.

AMANDA: Me too...

(Lights fade down on area 1, and fade up to same level on area 2, so that both areas are dimly lit... BRAD and CHERYL are naked on Brad's bed).

BRAD: ... Me too.

CHERYL: It's not as though I'm going to stay all night.

BUSTER: I want to stay with you. All night.

AMANDA: You can't.

BRAD: I want you to.

CHERYL: I can't.

BUSTER:	Why not?
AMANDA:	It'll be different when we've got our own place.
BRAD:	Tell you what. Why don't you move in with me?
CHERYL:	I couldn't. Not while, you know, I've got Amanda.
BUSTER:	What difference does it make.
AMANDA:	I want this to last. Not like her.
BRAD:	I won't ask you again, you know.
CHERYL:	That's all right, Brad. It's not as though we'll be together for ever (*she rises from the bed and begins to dress*).
AMANDA:	I want it to be forever. Just you and me, together forever.
BUSTER:	Sounds fine by me.
BRAD:	Fine. If that's the way you want it.
CHERYL:	I've got to... to have... my... my freedom.
BRAD:	To look for someone else, you mean.
AMANDA:	I'll never want anyone else but you.
BUSTER:	Let's keep it that way, huh? And maybe we can find somewhere more comfortable than this thing. Like a bed, maybe?
CHERYL:	So you want me to go?
BRAD:	I didn't say that.
CHERYL:	(*Angrily*) But that's what you meant, wasn't it. Wasn't it.
AMANDA:	If that's what you really want.
BUSTER:	I do.
BRAD:	If you say so.
AMANDA:	OK. She's not coming home. She'll stay the night at Brad's. We can use her double bed. How does that sound (*they slowly begin to get up from the couch*).
CHERYL:	(*Bitterly*) I don't mean a thing to you.

BRAD: You said it baby.

BUSTER: You said it. Great.

CHERYL: This is the end then.

BRAD: Guess so... if that's all it means to you.

AMANDA: Maybe this is the real beginning.

BUSTER: Maybe. Or maybe you shouldn't say that.

(BUSTER and AMANDA are slowly moving off R).

CHERYL: So... so I won't be coming round again.

BRAD: Just get out, willya. Go on... fuck off. I've had you. *(CHERYL slowly begins to move off L).*

AMANDA: Why not?

BUSTER: If there is a beginning, then there's got to be an end.

AMANDA: I don't care about the end. What we've got now is enough.

BUSTER: *(Slight pause)* Maybe.

(Lights quickly down on both areas).

MRS BOARDMAN WIDENS HER HORIZONS

Life can sometimes offer an unexpected surprise.

Cast: MRS BOARDMAN, a middle-aged cook/housekeeper, DOREEN, a sexy young parlourmaid.

Setting: The kitchen of the FitzGibbon mansion in Double Bay, Sydney. MRS BOARDMAN and DOREEN are in discussion.

DOREEN: Well now Mrs Boardman, what do we have to do with these spatchcocks?

BOARDMAN: All in good time, Doreen.

DOREEN: I suppose, now you've won the lottery, you'll be taking a holiday. If they let you.

BOARDMAN: Well they can't say I didn't tell them.

DOREEN: Ooh, I wish I'd been there.

BOARDMAN: Yairs. It was while she was doing the menu for tonight.

DOREEN: Go on! You told her in the middle of the menu!

BOARDMAN: Yairs. Of course he had to put his oar in. As usual. So I says to her, Madam, I've won the lottery.

DOREEN: Go on. You told her! Just like that!

BOARDMAN: Well I couldn't keep it to meself for ever, could I.

DOREEN: What'd she say?!

BOARDMAN: (*She says, mimicking*) Oh I think we'll have your herbed spatchcock tonight when the Walkers come to dinner. Just remember to ring up Churchill's the butcher and order them will you.

DOREEN: What! She never noticed?

BOARDMAN: Didn't raise an eyebrow. Went right over her head.

DOREEN: You'd think he would've cottoned on. That you're a millionaire.

BOARDMAN: Oh he never turned a hair neither.

DOREEN: Just goes to show.

BOARDMAN: So, what I thought, I'll give in my notice tomorrow night.

DOREEN: When you do them a cold supper.

BOARDMAN: Yes. In writing... in an henvelope.

DOREEN: Yes! On the supper tray!

BOARDMAN: Propped up, like, against the cruet.

DOREEN: Pity you won't be there to see it... (*gloats*) I will, but...

BOARDMAN: Not that I haven't enjoyed working with you, Doreen.

DOREEN: Whatcha gonna do with the money?

BOARDMAN: Well. There's that little house up in Queen Street.

DOREEN: What, the one for sale?

BOARDMAN: Not any longer.

DOREEN: Whatcha mean?

BOARDMAN: Thought I might put a deposit down on that.

DOREEN: No! You wouldn't!

BOARDMAN: Thought I might do a B & B up there.

DOREEN: Lodgers, you mean?

BOARDMAN: No... a bit more classy. You know... tourists.

DOREEN: What, Japs 'n that.

BOARDMAN: Well, we've had funnier than that here, at some o' them dinner parties.

DOREEN: You can say that again, Ugh! What about that Russian bloke, with the beard. Gawd it tickled.

BOARDMAN: I warned you. Stay away from him, I said, or you'll get more than you bargained for.

DOREEN: I did.

BOARDMAN: Yairs. Between the soup and the entree, wasn't it.

DOREEN:	What an appetite.
BOARDMAN:	And what about that Swede. You know, Swedish.
DOREEN:	Dirty bathtub. I don't take my clothes off for anybody.
BOARDMAN:	Yairs. I've had enough of them Contingnentals. That's why I think Japs.
DOREEN:	Yes... quiet like, usually, aren't they. Not ones to chase you down the passage.
BOARDMAN:	Though I'd miss having the big kitchen. And the cooker.
DOREEN:	Yeah, probly a bit pokey, up there in Queen Street.
BOARDMAN:	Not handy to the bus route, neither.
DOREEN:	Not like here.
BOARDMAN:	No. Makes you think.
DOREEN:	Yes. It's Convenience. Pshaw! Like that Russian bloke.
BOARDMAN:	How was he a convenience? A bloomin' inconvenience, I'd call him.
DOREEN:	No, what he wanted was A Convenience.
BOARDMAN:	You mean, after the soup?
DOREEN:	Yes. "Direct me to the convenience", he says to me when I took his soup plate away.
BOARDMAN:	So you showed him where the toilet is.
DOREEN:	I did. Though I never expected to go in there with him.
BOARDMAN:	Lucky you were back in time to serve the entree.
DOREEN:	Only just made it. Gawd he was fast.
BOARDMAN:	It takes all sorts.
DOREEN:	Y'know... that's what I like about you Mrs Boardman. You're tolerant.
BOARDMAN:	Have to be. To work here... for them.

DOREEN: Not long now, but, by the looks of it. Now you've got wealth.

BOARDMAN: Yairs... though it's a real bugger having to decide what to do with it.

DOREEN: Really? I thought you'd decided... you know, Queen Street?

BOARDMAN: Yairs... but what about if I have Second Thoughts.

DOREEN: Ooh! You'd never... would you?

BOARDMAN: I might.

DOREEN: Yes, but what would you do? Instead?

BOARDMAN: Well when you've got money, there's all sorts of things to do. Look at them. Always traipsing off on a World Cruise or some such.

DOREEN: Well... I wouldn't say no to a world cruise.

BOARDMAN: (*In a philosophical mood*) I always say, it does you good to Widen Your Horizons.

DOREEN: (lounging on the edge of the kitchen table with legs splayed) And there's be a lot to widen... on a World Cruise.

BOARDMAN: All that food...

DOREEN: Sailors.

BOARDMAN: You know, Doreen, I've always thought of you as refined.

DOREEN: Oh?

BOARDMAN: Cultured.

DOREEN: Well, I suppose...

BOARDMAN: Exposed to the Better Things in Life.

DOREEN: Well, you could say...

BOARDMAN: Willing to put yourself out.

DOREEN: Well I do like to...

BOARDMAN: And glamorous too.

DOREEN:	You think??
BOARDMAN:	Yairs... a bit of a hairdo... maybe a slinky black dress...
DOREEN:	Ooh! You mean like hers... that one that came the other day from David Jones...
BOARDMAN:	You've got a better figure.
DOREEN:	Really!?
BOARDMAN:	Yairs... you could go anywhere in a frock like that.
DOREEN:	(*Carried away*) Ooh! Couldn't I ever!
BOARDMAN:	All you'd need would be the chance.
DOREEN:	The opportunity.
BOARDMAN:	Like a World Cruise.
DOREEN:	Aw! If only...
BOARDMAN:	How about it.
DOREEN:	How about what?
BOARDMAN:	A World Cruise. You know... Hong Kong... the Philip-pines...
DOREEN:	Aw, go on...
BOARDMAN:	With a whole new wardrobe to go in.
DOREEN:	I'm never going near a wardrobe again.
BOARDMAN:	What?
DOREEN:	Not after that Swede got me inside that one in his bedroom... dirty bathtub...
BOARDMAN:	I don't mean a wardrobe. I mean a Wardrobe. You know... frocks 'n that.
DOREEN:	Like sexy underwear?
BOARDMAN:	You got it. Loungeray.
DOREEN:	Aw! Wow! If only...
BOARDMAN:	I mean it.
DOREEN:	You don't mean...

BOARDMAN: I do.

DOREEN: You and me! On a World Cruise?

BOARDMAN: That's what I said.

DOREEN: But what about Queen Street?

BOARDMAN: There's more to life than lodgers.

DOREEN: (*She realises*) You're serious!

BOARDMAN: I could book us in tomorrow.

DOREEN: I'm on! I'll give in my notice too! Same as you! On the supper tray!

BOARDMAN: In two henvelopes.

DOREEN: Propped up against the cruet! One each side, like!

BOARDMAN: Pity we won't be here to see it.

DOREEN: Ooh, what a shame.

BOARDMAN: Yairs. While they're wondering where their next hot dinner is coming from, you 'n me'll be lording it up in a honeymoon suite at the Hilton.

DOREEN: The Hilton! Well I never.

BOARDMAN: And we'll be on that cruise the next morning.

DOREEN: Yeah! With a cupla sailors maybe. One for you... and two for me.

BOARDMAN: Don't forget the Loungeray.

DOREEN: Yeah! Slinky like... with lace all over.

BOARDMAN: Doreen... I tell you what.

DOREEN: What?

BOARDMAN: You know that Ellen Degenerate they're all talking about.

DOREEN: What, the lesbinum? With, you know, the girlfriend?

BOARDMAN: I reckon, on the World Cruise, that'd be the way to go.

DOREEN: What? No sailors?

BOARDMAN: Oh yeah, we could get them on board later.

DOREEN: Well... at least I wouldn't have to get felt up in the wardrobe.

BOARDMAN: Be a pity to waste that sexy Loungeray.

DOREEN: I tell you what. Here's the deal. No facial hair. Not after that Russian.

BOARDMAN: No worries. I'll run over me face with the Veet.

DOREEN: Oh yeah. Much better than the wax.

BOARDMAN: But I tell you what. I do draw the line at doing one of them Brazilians.

DOREEN: Done... *(they shake hands)* Well! What do we do now.

BOARDMAN: Now?

DOREEN: Them spatchcocks I suppose.

BOARDMAN: Bugger the spatchcocks. Come on. Let's do our resignations.

(As they exit, MRS BOARDMAN gives DOREEN a playful smack on the bum; she squeals as the curtain falls.)

Frank Sutherland Davidson

BY THE SEA WALL

What can ease the pain of a wounded heart?

Cast: HE, *a troubled man,*
SHE, *a rescuer*

Setting: *A sea wall at the edge of a park overlooking the sea. Sounds of the sea crashing on rocks below the wall. If this were a film, a gardener cutting the grass with a motor mower would pass across the screen. At the wall, two people are standing near each other but not aware of each other, looking out front... to the sea. At first the dialogue is as though an exchange of thoughts.*

HE: Oh it's so grey...

SHE: It goes so far away...

HE: So grey...

SHE: That's not it...

HE: What?

SHE: The colour has nothing to do with it.

HE: I wasn't speaking...

SHE: I wasn't listening.

HE: Nobody listens... (*pause*) If they did they'd hear.

SHE: There's nobody to listen.

HE: No. Nobody.

SHE: It's better to do it this way?

HE: Yes. Easier.

SHE: Less painful.

HE: I don't care about pain. Not that sort.

SHE: (*Looking at him*) I don't know your name.

HE: I don't care.

SHE:	You should.
HE:	What's the point.
SHE:	I don't know. I just thought...
HE:	Don't bother me.
SHE:	You've got a look about you.
HE:	Don't mock me. I've had enough.
SHE:	I didn't mean...
HE:	I've got nothing about me. Nothing. There's nothing left.
SHE:	Not even inside?
HE:	Nothing. There's nothing there any more.
SHE:	There must be – something.
HE:	I'm so tired.
SHE:	Yes.
HE:	(*Shaking his head*) I can't do it. (*anguished*) Why can't I do it.
SHE:	You're brave enough.
HE:	What's that got to do with it.
SHE:	You would do it if you wanted to.
HE:	I'm so tired of being insulted.
SIIE:	I didn't mean...
HE:	Forget it.
SHE:	It's funny isn't it.
HE:	Funny.
SHE:	Yes.
HE:	No.
SHE:	I don't mean laughing funny.
HE:	No.
SHE:	I mean, I came here...

HE:	Can't you just leave me alone.
SHE:	I want to talk to you.
HE:	That's a joke.
SHE:	I came here because...
HE:	I want to be left alone. If you don't mind.
SHE:	Because once... I... I wanted to...
HE:	I'm too tired to listen.
SHE:	I wanted to... just walk into the sea...
HE:	(*He looks at her... probably for the first time*) From here you don't walk. You jump.
SHE:	Is that what...
HE:	(*Savagely*) You jump.
SHE:	What's funny is... that time... all I could see was the distance. All stretched out... going on forever.
HE:	You're a fraud.
SHE:	No.
HE:	Nobody knows what it's like.
SHE:	Do they tell you to 'pull yourself together'?
HE:	What?
SHE:	They tell you to 'snap out of it'?
HE:	Who are you?
SHE:	It doesn't matter.
HE:	People used to matter. Names used to matter... now... it's just... grey... everywhere...
SHE:	You mean the sea.
HE:	I mean everything I see. My soul. Everything.
SHE:	You want to sink into the greyness? The greyness of the sea?
HE:	You know everything don't you.
SHE:	That's what I wanted.

HE:	Why don't you do it then. I won't stop you.
SHE:	Maybe one day I will have to. Unless...
HE:	Unless what.
SHE:	It doesn't matter.
HE:	I suppose not.
SHE:	Unless I 'pull myself together'.
HE:	Unless you 'snap out of it'. (*He begins to laugh in a manner that is soon transformed into a fit of weeping*).
SHE:	Is that what they say to you.
HE:	(*He has subsided into a crumpled heap and says brokenly*) This is not me. I'm better than this.
SHE:	It's like an insurance policy, isn't it.
HE:	What are you talking about
SHE:	(*Gesturing*) It's like a comfort you can always return to..
HE:	This place.
SHE:	The place where you would do it... if you were going to do it.
HE:	When. Not if... when.
SHE:	When you do it.
HE:	Not with people around.
SHE:	People matter.
HE:	No.
SHE:	There are people who care.
HE:	To care... you have to understand.
SHE:	I do... (*pause*).
HE:	You came here to... you said...
SHE:	So did you.
HE:	It didn't work... this time.
SHE:	No.

HE: (*Angrily*) I suppose you think you've rescued me.

SHE: No-one else can rescue you... only yourself.

HE: Why would I bother.

SHE: You don't need to punish yourself.

HE: Living is the punishment. Just living is the agony that never stops.

SHE: Sometimes... you meet someone... when you least expect it... someone who does understand.

HE: Nobody.

SHE: What?

HE: Nobody understands.

SHE: While you tell yourself that nobody understands... you'll never find anybody who does.

HE: There's nowhere else to look. Only here.

SHE: Maybe... that's the reason I'm here.

HE: I don't know you.

SHE: Sometimes that helps.

HE: Oh you're so clever. Tell me... go on, tell me. What's wrong with me.

SHE: Yes. You're severely depressed. You think that ending it is the only way you can escape the pain of it. You desperately want oblivion.

HE: I'm too tired to care.

SHE: You see the sea... the grey sea... as the blanket that will cover you... that will warm you into death. And then you will know no more. It will all be over.

HE: Why are you interfering. Why couldn't I just take that step... one jump...

SHE: That's what I was going to do. Once. Not so long ago. Oh not here... on the beach, down there... I wanted to walk into the water and never think again, never feel anything again...

HE:	And you didn't do it.
SHE:	No.
HE:	No?
SHE:	No. It was then that someone came... a stranger... and spoke to me. And he knew. He understood the way I felt. He'd once felt the same, he said. And he said... I can still hear him saying it... he said "Now I come down here to the beach to prove to myself how strong I have made myself." It didn't make sense to me then... but I understand it now.
HE:	I haven't the strength.
SHE:	What you haven't got is the capacity to love yourself. You have let yourself dry up inside. That's why you think there's nothing there. But there is. There is. You need to tell yourself that.
HE:	Tell myself... what?
SHE:	Tell yourself... I am a good person. I am a strong person. I have a strength that noone else can understand. My strength is my goodness. My goodness is my strength."
HE:	You're mad.
SHE:	The capacity to love is endless, and that love must include yourself. Love doesn't start from the outside... it starts from the inside. If you don't love your own spirit, your spirit will die... just as yours is trying to do... because you have starved it of the love it needs.
HE:	You think this is all my fault.
SHE:	No. There is no fault. There is no blame.
HE:	No. There is only agony and death.
SHE:	Or love and life. You can choose. Choose something you have loved. Anything. No matter how simple; no matter how small.
HE:	I... I can't.
SHE:	Forget the pain... for just a minute. Think. Think

	of something you once loved... something you once enjoyed...
HE:	*(With painful hesitation)* When the new grass was cut - I always loved the scent of new-mown grass.
SHE:	Sit here with me. We will smell it together.

(She turns him to face inward. She sits and indicates for him to join her. He sits. Now with their backs to the sea wall, they breathe together as though meditating... Gradually his head inclines to her shoulder, hers to his.

(As they rest together, the lights fade).

TROUBLE ON NOAH'S ARK

A re-interpretation...

Cast: MR NOAH, *of Bible fame*
MRS NOAH, *his wife*
MR PIG }
MR SNAKE } *animal passengers*
MS MONKEY }

Setting: *Noah's Ark. MR NOAH and MRS NOAH are together on deck.*

MR NOAH: The water's still on the rise. Where will it stop, I wonder.

MRS NOAH: Don't worry dear. We've got all the creatures on board now, just as God said, so I'm sure all will be well.

MR NOAH: That may be but God didn't give us any instructions about stabling and how do I know whether we've got all the right foods?

MRS NOAH: Well those lions are a bit of a worry.

(Sounds of lions roaring)

MRS NOAH: That's why I sneaked a few extra pigs on board.

MR NOAH: Mrs Noah! You don't mean to tell me that you disobeyed God. He distinctly told me...

MRS NOAH: Yes, yes, I know what he said. Two by two. Without any instruction at all about eating provisions, let alone the segregation of the species. As well as sending us this rotten flood, he's left all the finer aspects of the arrangements to us. So that's why...

MR NOAH: We were supposed to take on board only one male and one female of each species...

MRS NOAH: That's all very well but who's got to decide where to put them all? We can't have the cats and the dogs sharing the same cage, and as for the hippopotamuses...

MR NOAH:	Hippopotami.
MRS NOAH:	Hippopot-am-I what.
MR NOAH:	Hippopotami. It's plural. One hippopotamus, hippopotamus. Two hippopotamuses, hippopotami.
MRS NOAH:	Oh, hippopotamus schmitopotamus, who cares already.
MR NOAH:	God cares. That's why we're here.
MRS NOAH:	If only we didn't have to leave our lovely little wattle-and-daub hut...
MR NOAH:	What! This is a much better erection.
MRS NOAH:	Yes, that's another thing...
MR NOAH:	*(Hurriedly interrupting)* One of my better erections...
MRS NOAH:	Yes well I certainly hope you can make it last longer than usual.
MR NOAH:	Don't you worry, dear. God has told me it's going to last for forty days and forty nights.
MRS NOAH:	Did he now. Well at least that's something to look forward to.
MR NOAH:	And meanwhile, we've got to solve the problem of how to feed all these creatures.
MRS NOAH:	Yes, and stop them from tearing each other to pieces.
MR NOAH:	I wish you'd stop worrying dear. You know that the Lord will provide.
MRS NOAH:	Well if he's anything like me, he just might forget something that's needed, and we can hardly be expected to nip out to the corner shop if we run out of whatever it is.
MR NOAH:	Oh, the corner shop will have been inundated ages ago.
MRS NOAH:	What does it matter. If it's not there, it's not there.
	(More sounds of lions roaring)
MR NOAH:	The lions are sounding very hungry. I'd better go and do something about it.

MRS NOAH:	Hallo! Something's coming up the ladder from the hold.

(MR PIG ENTERS)

MR PIG:	Phew... *(honk)* That's a hard climb for a pig.
MRS NOAH:	Yes, I would have preferred a lift myself, but you know what these tradesmen are like.
MR PIG:	Oh, absolutely... *(honk honk)* You should have seen the pigsty we left behind. It was an absolute... pigsty.
MR NOAH:	Just be grateful that God has seen fit to preserve your species.
MR PIG:	That's another thing. I thought the terms of the arrangement were that me and Mabel were the only two to get a billet on this ark. What do I find? *(honk honk honk)* There's a whole consignment of porkers down below, snorting and farting like there's no tomorrow.
MRS NOAH:	Oh you won't be troubled by them for long. It's the lions' feeding time now, *(to MR NOAH)* isn't it dear.
MR NOAH:	Shush, dear. We don't want to deplete our supplies all at once.

(MR SNAKE has entered)

MR PIG:	Well whatever you're going to do about it, just get on with it.
MR SNAKE:	Only too happy to be of assissssstance.

(MR SNAKE gobbles up MR PIG who despite loud noises of protest is soon completely devoured)

MRS NOAH:	There. What did I tell you. Aren't you glad I thought of bringing those extra porkers.
MR NOAH:	This is going to completely bugger up the ark manifest.
MR SNAKE:	That was an extremely satisfying firsssst courssssse. If you don't mind, I'll hibernate now for a week or two. Just wake me up when it's time for desssssert.

(MR SNAKE curls up and goes to sleep)

MR NOAH: This is all your fault. I might have known those courses you did in Resource Management would go to your head.

MRS NOAH: Don't blame me. If God had been a bit more organised we wouldn't be in this pickle.

(MS MONKEY jumps down from the rigging)

MS MONKEY: Did someone mention pickles?

MRS NOAH: Oh no. Not another special meal request. This is worse than working for Qantas.

MR NOAH: You've never worked for Qantas in your life.

MS MONKEY: Bring on the pickles, I say. I'll have a few nuts to go with them, too.

MRS NOAH: *(Hotly)* You'll do no such thing.

MR NOAH: Now calm down you two. This ark depends on mutual cooperation.

MS MONKEY: Did you say mutual fornication? I wouldn't mind a bit of that, to go with the nuts.

MRS NOAH: You need your ears washed out.

MR NOAH: The bathing schedule hasn't been devised yet *(grumbling)* That's another bloody thing that god's forgotten...

MS MONKEY: Ah, don't worry about it. We'll all go communal.

MRS NOAH: Not on my ark you won't.

MR NOAH: Your ark? Don't forget it's my erection.

MRS NOAH: Yes and a fat lot of good it is. Animals all over the place, no regular feeding times... these creatures'll be running the whole show soon if you don't show a bit of resourcefulness.

MR NOAH: Whinge whinge whinge. Why don't you do something useful.

MRS NOAH: Like what?

MR NOAH: Like doing a roll call. We have to know exactly who we've got on board now, after all this disruption.

MRS NOAH: Great. I'll start here. PIG! *(there is a series of muffled grunts from inside the Snake)*... MONKEY!

MS MONKEY: Use your eyes you old Bat, I'm right here in front of you and if you can't see me ....

MRS NOAH: *(Bellowing over MONKEY'S line)* SNAKE!!!

MR SNAKE: *(Waking up)* AHHH! Dessert!!! *(he seizes MONKEY and devours her with great effort, despite her protests which gradually fade as she disappears)*

MR NOAH: Oh my goodness. Now the manifest is really buggered. The animals came by twos and twos, but when they leave there'll be odd numbers all over the place...

MR SNAKE: *(Having had a few burps during Mr Noah's last speech)* Would you like me to assssssssissst?

MR NOAH: Could you?

MR SNAKE: I'd be delighted. Now. Which of you would like to go first?

MR NOAH: Go first? What do you mean?

MRS NOAH: He means us, numbskull. I'm going up the frigging rigging.
(SNAKE with great difficulty wriggles towards MR NOAH, while MRS NOAH disappears up the rigging).

MR NOAH: Right. That's enough. Hold everything *(SNAKE halts, unable to move)* I'm not having gluttony aboard my ark. Regurgitate.

SNAKE: What!

MR NOAH: Immediately. Come on... out with it. I mean, them.

SNAKE: What a spoilsport *(begins to cough up)*.

MR NOAH: I'm not having any more mixing of the species. *(MONKEY reappears)* Now get back to wherever you were allocated, and mind your own business.

MONKEY: Glad to. Anything's better than sharing with a pig *(MONKEY goes up the rigging).*

MR NOAH: Come on; next one *(SNAKE coughs up PIG)* And as for you... I've a good mind to feed you to the lions.

PIG:	Lay a hand on my bacon and you'll have my Mabel to contend with (*honk*).
MR NOAH:	Don't argue; down the hatch, and make it speedy.
PIG:	(*Going*) Can't wait to get a good bit of dirt to have a good root around in.
MR NOAH:	(*To SNAKE*) Right. Let's get a few things straight. What's your justification for having your name on the manifest?
SNAKE:	Eh?
MR NOAH:	You heard. Why did God give you permission to come on board the ark? What's so special about the Snake species?
SNAKE:	Haven't you read the manifest?
MR NOAH:	I can't be expected to remember everything --
SNAKE:	It seems to me that you're a bit backward with the Scriptures.
MR NOAH:	Yes, well, I have to admit, I usually leave that sort of thing to Mrs Noah. After all... I'm only a mere male.
SNAKE:	That's right... blame the woman. Haven't you heard of Equal Opportunity?
MR NOAH:	Frequently. Ever since she did that blasted Resource Management course.
SNAKE:	Well. Don't you reckon it might be time for us males to... you know... team up?
MR NOAH:	Ooh! Now I remember. You're being preserved so that in the future, post-flood you know, mankind will still have to suffer Temptation, and try to avoid the sin of giving in to it.
SNAKE:	Got it in one. And now I'm going back below, to rest up for the new world order (*EXITS*).
MR NOAH:	If only I could have fed him to the lions. Oh well...
MRS NOAH:	(*OFF*) Yoo hoo! Mr Noah! Are you still on deck?
MR NOAH:	Yes dear. What is it?

MRS NOAH: (*ENTERS*) Well, dear, that nice Mrs Monkey has given me a bag of her special nuts for us to try. I've just had one and they're delicious (*holds out bag*).

MR NOAH: Well... the Scriptures did warn us about apples, but I don't remember anything about giving in to nuts, so... (*he takes a nut and eats it*)

SNAKE: (*APPEARING*) Well done. Mrs Noah!

MRS NOAH: What!

SNAKE: You've just guaranteed my job for the post-flood reconstruction era.

MR NOAH: You mean...

SNAKE: Yesssss! I shall remain the living symbol of temptation (*EXITS*).

MRS NOAH: Well there's not much we can do about that. I'm going off to feed the lions (*EXITS*).

MR NOAH: I must say, those nuts were pretty good. Well... time to set sail for the future... with whatever trials and tribulations are coming with us (*calls over the side*) Anchors away!

(*Music swells... Lights fade... END*)

Frank Sutherland Davidson

MARLEEN'S WEDDING

Mother doesn't always know what's best...

Cast: *MUM, a nice middle-aged woman,*
MARLEEN, her daughter, and good-natured slapper.

Setting: *Mum's living room, where MUM is sitting doing some darning. Enter MARLEEN.*

MUM: Hello love. You're home early.

MARLEEN: Got some news for you Mum.

MUM: Go on! Hope it's good.

MARLEEN: Oh it's good all right.

MUM: Don't tell me you've got a new boyfriend.

MARLEEN: Nah. Anyway, what's wrong with Ben.

MUM: Oh... nothing... except... well...

MARLEEN: Well what?

MUM: Marleen... you've been going together for five years. Isn't it time he... you know... isn't it time you both... I mean...

MARLEEN: Told ya I had some news.

MUM: You... you don't mean...

MARLEEN: Yeah. Ben'n I've decided to get a place of our own. Move in together.

MUM: (*Disappointed*) Oh. Oh, for a minute I thought you meant...

MARLEEN: Yeah. That too.

MUM: You mean...

MARLEEN: Yep. We're gonna get hitched.

MUM: MARRIED! Oh, Marleen... (*hugs her*) Oh that's lovely Marleen. Even if it is Ben.

MARLEEN:	What's wrong with Ben!
MUM:	Oh! Nothing... nothing at all... now!
MARLEEN:	Gawd, Mum, you're a real wedding junkie.
MUM:	Oh I've been longing for this day. There'll be such a lot to think about, everything to arrange...
MARLEEN:	Steady on Mum.
MUM:	There'll be the church to decide on... and the flowers...
MARLEEN:	Hold on Mum. We're not havin' a church.
MUM:	What?
MARLEEN:	Nah. Ben 'n me, we thought we might just go in to the Court House in Liverpool, but now we've got a better idea...
MUM:	The Court House! Oh Marleen! They don't even have an organ...
MARLEEN:	I don't want any more organ than what I'm gettin' already.
MUM:	At least you have to have a proper wedding dress.
MARLEEN:	I tell you, Mum, I'd rather decide meself. I'm gonna do something none of the other girls have ever done.
MUM:	Ooh! What is it? Is it expensive?
MARLEEN:	Not if I use that material you got for the curtains.
MUM:	(*Aghast*) You surely don't want to get married in a pair of curtains.
MARLEEN:	I won't need much. You'll still have enough for one winder.
MUM:	Yes but I've got two windows remember.
MARLEEN:	It's my wedding. And you've already got the material.
MUM:	Yes but it's not suitable! It's see-through.
MARLEEN:	So?!

MUM: You don't want everybody looking up your....

MARLEEN: Get with it Mum. That's what everybody's doing.

MUM: I just think... you know... if you show too much...

MARLEEN: Too much what?

MUM: Well, you're going to look... you know...

MARLEEN: What??

MUM: Well... a bit worn.

MARLEEN: Christ, Mum, it's new material! Isn't it? You haven't used it already have you?

MUM: You want to look as though you've just got out of bed?

MARLEEN: Well I will of.

MUM: I mean with him.

MARLEEN: Get real Mum. I'm not havin' the bloody weddin' at the bedside. I'm not havin' Dad sayin' the bloody girl couldn't even get out of bed to go to her own weddin'. You know what he's like.

MUM: Oh I do. More's the pity. Give him an inch...and he'll take a mile.

MARLEEN: Eh? Anyway. What did you wear at your wedding.

MUM: Oh I had a lovely frock, real elegant it was, I had it on lay-by for weeks.

MARLEEN: Lay-by? (*chuckles*) What sort of a lay's that? Sounds like it could be fun.

MUM: Not that sort of lay.

MARLEEN: Oh.

MUM: No. In those days we had to save up for what we wanted.

MARLEEN: Sounds like a bloody stupid idea.

MUM: It might sound stupid to you. But it wasn't.

MARLEEN: You mean you and Dad never had sex? Before the wedding?

MUM: Oh that was different.
MARLEEN: How?
MUM: That was Romance.
MARLEEN: I don't see the difference. A shag's a shag.
MUM: It got different when it got legal.
MARLEEN: You mean it got better?
MUM: Well... in some ways... in others it got worse.
MARLEEN: Worse?
MUM: Well... for one thing... I had you.
MARLEEN: You mean... you didn't want to have me?
MUM: Well... I did and I didn't.
MARLEEN: Bloody lovely. Here I am, just about to marry Ben, and I find out I was never wanted.
MUM: I wasn't ready for it.
MARLEEN: Why?
MUM: It was too soon.
MARLEEN: Well why'd you get fuckin' pregnant then.
MUM: It was accidental.
MARLEEN: So now I'm an accident.
MUM: Oh dear. It seems to me that life's just one accident after another.
MARLEEN: Yeah. Call the bloody ambulance.
MUM: That's why I want you to have a proper wedding dress.
MARLEEN: Proper? What'cha mean proper?
MUM: So it doesn't look like, you know, an accident.
MARLEEN: I'm not having an outfit where you can't show your boobs.
MUM: That's what I'm afraid of, that see-through material.

MARLEEN:	Oh I won't need it for that. That'll be me train. You know, out behind. I'll be showin' all me front. I want everyone to see what Ben's gettin'.
MUM:	Seems to me he's been getting it already.
MARLEEN:	Jealous, are you, Mum?
MUM:	Don't be silly Marleen. You don't seem to realize. Your wedding day should be something to look back on. Something nice.
MARLEEN:	Yeah. It will be. I'm gonna be really OUT THERE.
MUM:	It would be a lot nicer if...
MARLEEN:	If what?
MUM:	If you let me get you a really nice wedding dress. I'd pay for it you know.
MARLEEN:	Really?
MUM:	Yes, I've got it saved up. We could go to that Bridal Salon in Harris Park...
MARLEEN:	Tell you what Mum.
MUM:	What?
MARLEEN:	We'll go to this bloody saloon of yours.
MUM:	You mean it?
MARLEEN:	Yeah. We can go there, and get you a nice frock to wear at the wedding.
MUM:	But I wanted...
MARLEEN:	Mum, I'm tryin' to tell you...
MUM:	You mean you've really made up your mind?
MARLEEN:	Sure have. And so has Ben.
MUM:	I just hope you won't show... everything... I'll just die...
MARLEEN:	No need to peg out just yet, Mum.
MUM:	Why?
MARLEEN:	Well. Ben wants a nude wedding.

MUM:	What?
MARLEEN:	Yeah. He's found this nude celebrant down in the Shire that does them.
MUM:	Oh no...
MARLEEN:	In the garden.
MUM:	Not our garden.
MARLEEN:	That's the idea.
MUM:	But the neighbours...
MARLEEN:	We've been round the lot and asked them all and only one of 'em said she wouldn't come. Bloody old Mrs Greenough.

(MUM has a decided change of attitude)

MUM:	What? After all she put us through with that bikie gang of hers?
MARLEEN:	Yeah. Buncha wankers.
MUM:	Oh. The hide of her.
MARLEEN:	You said it Mum.
MUM:	Oh dear. I've a good mind to…
MARLEEN:	What?
MUM:	Tell you what Marleen.
MARLEEN:	Eh?
MUM:	That money I saved up for that dress...
MARLEEN:	Yeah?
MUM:	How about we go down to Dan Murphy's and order a few crates of champagne.
MARLEEN:	Aw! Beaudy bottler!
MUM:	And get a band. A loud one.
MARLEEN:	Hey, wow! Great idea Mum. But what about your new frock?
MUM:	Bugger it Marleen. If it's a nude wedding... I don't want to stand out like a sore thumb.

MARLEEN: No way. So what you gonna do.

MUM: I'll strip off just in time for the vows.

MARLEEN: That's more like it Mum.

MUM: (*Briskly*) Yes. Now. You'll want your father to give you away.

MARLEEN: Oh gawd. Here we go again.

MUM: He'll have to be in the nude too of course. Oh dear. Whatever are we going to do about his beer gut.

MARLEEN: Well... a few weeks on that Jenny Craig might do the trick.

MUM: (*Snaps fingers*) I'll get him signed up right away... Soon's he wakes up...

MARLEEN: Yeah... get the ol' bastard outa bed... (*they EXIT*).

ONE IN THE BATH

What happens might not be what's expected.

Cast: JASMINE, *the next door neighbour*
MELINDA, *the other neighbour*
JASON, *an eligible bachelor.*

Setting: *Two flats, indicated by spots. A telephone is ringing in one flat.*

(MELINDA holds a telephone; in the other, JASMINE is about to answer. MELINDA has by her a brown paper grocery bag with shopping in it).

JASMINE:	Hello?
MELINDA:	Jas? It's... it's Mel.
JASMINE:	Hi! You sound stressed. What's happened?
MELINDA:	I... I just got home...
JASMINE:	Yes? Well?
MELINDA:	I went to go to the loo... and... oh...
JASMINE:	What!
MELINDA:	There's a man in the bath. I think he's dead.
JASMINE:	What!
MELINDA:	He's naked.
JASMINE:	What!
MELINDA:	In the bath.
JASMINE:	Really naked?
MELINDA:	Yes!
JASMINE:	Are you sure he's dead?
MELINDA:	I think so. He didn't move.
JASMINE:	What are you going to do!

MELINDA:	I don't know!
JASMINE:	(*After a pause*) Who is it.
MELINDA:	(*Slightly hysterical*) What do you mean who is it, I don't know who it is.
JASMINE:	Well didn't you ask?
MELINDA:	I'm really stressed out. Couldn't you come over?
JASMINE:	I could... but you see, I'm expecting someone.
MELINDA:	Expecting someone.
JASMINE:	Yeah. A blind date in fact.
MELINDA:	You don't seem to realize... I've got a dead man in my bath. I just don't know what to do...
JASMINE:	(*Reassuringly*) Look Mel, normally I'd be over there in a flash. Make you a coffee or something. But...
MELINDA:	A coffee! Is that all you can think about.
JASMINE:	No, that's what I'm saying. I'm expecting a blind date, and I don't want to be out when he calls.
MELINDA:	Oh god. I'm going to hyperventilate.
JASMINE:	Have you got a paper bag?
MELINDA:	A fat lot you care (*empties groceries onto floor, uses paper bag*).
JASMINE:	Well have you?
MELINDA:	(*Between puffs*) If you... really cared... you'd be over here... I might be... murdered at the telephone...
JASMINE:	You mean you've got a murderer in the flat? With you?
MELINDA:	Oh god. I'm going to faint.
JASMINE:	Stick your head between your knees...
MELINDA:	(*Still puffing*) What... do you... think I am a... contortionist... ?
JASMINE:	Just be careful not to fall off the chair. You could break something...

MELINDA: A lot you care...

JASMINE: Look, Mel, just listen, listen...

MELINDA: (*Head between knees, still puffing*) If I'm murdered... it'll be all your fault...

JASMINE: Mel, if you've got a dead man in the bath, and he's dead, there's nothing he can do to you, right?

MELINDA: How do I know.

JASMINE: Why don't you go back to the bathroom, and hold a mirror over his nose...

MELINDA: What good will that do? He won't be able to see anything.

JASMINE: I don't mean for him to look at. I mean to see if he's breathing.

MELINDA: Of course he isn't breathing. He's dead, I tell you.

JASMINE: Yes, but you've got to be sure before you ring the police.

MELINDA: The police?

JASMINE: Of course... you've got to call the police. You can't go round with a dead man in your bath forever, you know.

MELINDA: I don't even know who he is.

JASMINE: How did he get in anyway? Did you leave the door open?

MELINDA: Of course I didn't.

JASMINE: Are you sure?

MELINDA: Of course I'm sure. I never leave the door open.

JASMINE: Well he must have had a key then. Who else has got a key to your flat?

MELINDA: No-one. Only the agent...

JASMINE: Well, it might be the agent.

MELINDA: What, in the bath?

JASMINE: Maybe he felt hot. And just got in the bath, you know, to cool down...

MELINDA: (*Outraged*) What, without asking first? I don't think so.

JASMINE: ... and went to sleep, and drowned. It has been known.

MELINDA: Well it would serve him right. I wonder if it is the agent...

JASMINE: Has he left a business card?

MELINDA: How would I know.

JASMINE: Well, have a look!

MELINDA: He hasn't left anything. Just a pile of clothes on the floor.

JASMINE: Have a look in his pockets then. There'll be something... a driver's license, maybe, or a credit card with his name on it...

MELINDA: I can't go poking around in his clothes.

JASMINE: Look, Mel, I'd do it for you, if only I could come over... but I can't.

MELINDA: (*Grimly*) So you said. I won't forget this, Jas.

JASMINE: If it was any other day...

MELINDA: (*Getting increasingly worked up*) Oh, excuse me. I'll just go in and wave my magic wand over him, will I, and bring him back to life and tell him to come back and die in the bath tomorrow, when it suits you.

JASMINE: I didn't mean...

MELINDA: Because you're too busy to be bothered to come over, even when I've been made into a crime scene...

JASMINE: Look, I've told you...

MELINDA: Yeah. I know. Blind date. Tell you what.. Why don't you come over and have a dead date with this one...

JASMINE: Mel... don't be stupid...

MELINDA:	... while you're waiting for the other one. Take him off my hands...
JASMINE:	If only I wasn't expecting...
MELINDA:	... out of my bath...
JASMINE:	Look Mel, this guy I've got coming, I've seen his photo. His name's Jason and he's gorgeous. I just don't want to miss seeing him...
MELINDA:	Well mine's gorgeous too.
JASMINE:	What do you mean. I thought you said he was dead.
MELINDA:	He is.
JASMINE:	You know what Mel? If I was you, I'd ring the ambulance... They're really good in a crisis... they'd do a dead body for you, for sure.
	(Door to MELINDA's bathroom opens. ENTER JASON, wet hair and dressed in MELINDA's bathrobe.)
	(MELINDA gasps and drops telephone).
JASMINE:	*(Curious rather than worried)* Mel!. Mel! Are you all right?
JASON:	It's OK, honey.
MELINDA:	You're dead...
JASON:	*(Laughs)* Not by a long shot. Anyway... if I was, the sight of you'd bring me back... in a flash!
JASMINE:	Mel! Can you hear me Mel!!
MEL.INDA:	Are you sure you're not dead?
JASON:	Want me to prove it? *(undoes bathrobe, flash).*
MELINDA:	*(Impressed)* How did you get in?
JASON:	That agent guy in the office gave me your key. Said, that you said, that if I got here early, I could come in and make myself at home. Well, I reckoned...
MELINDA:	So you had a bath... in my bathroom.
JASON:	Sure did, honey... just in case, you know, you'd like

	me all freshened up.
MELINDA:	Bloody cheek.
JASMINE:	Mel! If you don't answer, I'm putting the phone down. Jason'll be here at any minute...
JASON:	Nice bathroom.
MELINDA:	Just a minute. What's you name.
JASON:	Why, Jasmine... you know already what it is. Don't you? Didn't they tell you?
MELINDA:	I'm not Jasmine. She lives in the other flat. I'm Melinda.
JASON:	What!
MELINDA:	You didn't happen to be on a blind date, did you... Jason?
JASON:	Hey... that's more like it. At least you can remember my name.
MELINDA:	Just a minute.

(MELINDA returns to the phone).

MELINDA:	Are you still there, Jas?
JASMINE:	Yeah... thank god, you sound all right now... what's happened?
MELINDA:	Oh nothing... just a case of mistaken identity... and hey... Jas... good luck with the blind date!
JASMINE:	Oh, gee, thanks Mel. Well, if you're sure you're OK... Goodbye.
MELINDA:	Goodbye!
JASON:	Hey... Maybe I'd better go and put my clothes back on...
MELINDA:	Hey... what's the hurry... I kinda like you the way you are...
JASON:	What! No kidding! Cool!
MELINDA:	In fact, I was thinking of slipping into something a

little loose myself... (*perhaps showing a shoulder*).

(*MELINDA comes closer to JASON, who opens bathrobe... or perhaps slips it off completely, and embraces her; they go into a pash, while in JASMINE'S flat, JASMINE looks disconsolately at her watch as the lights fade*).

JASMINE: Where the hell is Jason?

END

Frank Sutherland Davidson

JUSTIN'S FIRST ASSIGNMENT

A farce in one scene.

Cast: JUSTIN, *earnest cub reporter from a suburban newspaper,*
HITLER, *as Hitler,*
EVA, *Eva Braun, Hitler's mistress,*
CHURCHILL, *the Prime Minister of the UK.*

Setting: Hell... HITLER *is lounging by the cocktail cabinet. There is a KNOCK on the door.*

HITLER: Ach! Herein!

(ENTER JUSTIN, a cub reporter).

JUSTIN: Bloody hot down here... *(tentatively)* I'm Justin?

HITLER: Vat you vant?

JUSTIN: Well... my editor's just told me to go to hell, so I've come down to find somebody to interview. It's my first assignment... for the Human Interest page.

(JUSTIN looks closely at HITLER).

JUSTIN: I say... you aren't... are you... by any chance... actually... Hitler?

HITLER: Ach! You are from zee Press, no?

JUSTIN: Yes. The Wentworth Courier, actually.

HITLER: Gott im Himmel! Vot iss ziss Ventvorse Courier?

JUSTIN: It's a suburban.

HITLER: Ach! Iss goot. My best support it koms from zee suburbans.

JUSTIN: Well I'm not actually here to offer you support, Mr Hitler.

HITLER: *(Furious)* HERR Hitler.

JUSTIN: What!?

HITLER: You vill address me as Herr Hitler.

JUSTIN:	Oh... OK!
HITLER:	(*Demonstrating*) Und you vill salute.
JUSTIN:	Salute?
HITLER:	Ya... (*peering in sinister fashion*) You are not yet a member of zee Hitler Youth?
JUSTIN:	I'd rather not comment.
HITLER:	Ach. You are Juden, nein.
JUSTIN:	No, I'm Australian.
HITLER:	Alvays they send me zee Juden. I tell you, it is Hell.
JUSTIN:	Yes! It's supposed to be... isn't it? Isn't that why you're here? You know... the Holocaust and so on.
HITLER:	Vot do they know.
JUSTIN:	Well... everyone knows that you caused millions of deaths...
HITLER:	For zee Fatherland I did it.
JUSTIN:	Look, I'm not here to debate it with you. I want to get a real human interest story. Couldn't we just settle down and let me ask you a few questions?
HITLER:	I do not speak visout a vitness.
JUSTIN:	Well haven't you got any friends down here? What about Himmler, or Goering perhaps.
HITLER:	Ha ha ha. You sink I believe anysink Goering says?
JUSTIN:	If you really have to have a witness, I just thought...
HITLER:	I call Eva.
JUSTIN:	Eva Braun! Is she here too?
HITLER:	She accompanies me on my journey into Lust.
JUSTIN:	Crikey! That's a bit of human interest. Have you got very far with it? Lust, I mean?
HITLER:	It is unsatisfactory. Zere is no blood.
JUSTIN:	Oh... golly. I thought lust was just... well... you know...
HITLER:	Vot I seek is zee Blood Lust. I must have blood to achieve zee satisfactory climax.

JUSTIN: Crumbs! Isn't that going to be a bit hard... when you're more or less... you know... incorporeal?

HITLER: (*In a rage*) You vill not address me as Corporal! I am zee Fuhrer, Zee all-powerful, zee leader of zee Aryan people, zee Father of Chermany...

JUSTIN: OK, OK... calm down...

HITLER: Corporal! Pah! I spit on you (*he spits*).

JUSTIN: (*Dodging*) Maybe we should get Eva in here.

HITLER: She komms at my command... (*he calls*) EVA! EVA! Komm here. Schnell.

(*ENTER EVA. She wears a one-piece bathing costume in '30's style*)

EVA: Mein libeling Adolphie. Vot is your pleasure.

HITLER: Ach. Komm here mein liddle lusty-poo und I give you smacking und kiss.

(*HITLER kisses EVA while smacking her behind. JUSTIN writes in his notebook*).

JUSTIN: Apparently... Hitler still enjoys... quasi-sadistic lovemaking.

EVA: Und now mein libeling...

HITLER: Ach. Now ve dispose of ziss Juden.

JUSTIN: (*Writing*) His persecution... of Jury... still seems... entrenched in his psyche...

EVA: Ah ha! But first!... zee cocktail hour.

JUSTIN: How amazing! They seem to have adopted the American habit of serving cocktails. (*as he writes*) I suppose that's a result of the American occupation of Berlin.

HITLER: I vill have zee Cherry Brandy. It is red... like zee blood, ha ha ha.

EVA: I vill serve you mein Fuhrer. Und then... we drink together to zee Fatherland.

JUSTIN: (*Still writing*) Hell doesn't seem to have dimmed their devotion to their delusion.

HITLER:	Und then. I perform for you ze Bavarian folk dance in ze leiderhosen.
EVA:	Vile I sunbake mein desirable body on ze terrace
HITLER:	Und zen we roll naked in ze daisies...
JUSTIN:	Crickey! Wish I'd brought a camera. This is going to drive my editor wild…
EVA:	Consumed by ze Grand Passion!

(They embrace wildly until HITLER purposefully releases EVA).

HITLER:	Eva... serve ze Juden. Viss ze Berchestgarten cocktail! ha ha ha
EVA:	As alvays I obey mein Fuhrer.

(EVA mixes drinks at the cocktail cabinet).

JUSTIN:	*(Still writing)* Hitler's carnal desires still seem to function here in Hell... but is he able to realise his intentions?
HITLER:	Ach, it is goot. Even here my work for Chermany continues. Zee Third Reich lives.
JUSTIN:	Are you sure about that? Didn't you commit suicide?
HITLER:	Vat of it. Here are all zee comforts of zee bunker, *(cannily)* Und zee enemy never gets any closer.
JUSTIN:	That's because they've all gone up to the other place. Mostly.
HITLER:	*(Peering suspiciously at him)* Zat may be. Except for Churchill.
JUSTIN:	What, is he here too?
HITLER:	*(Evasively)* He wisits.
JUSTIN:	He visits you... here?
HITLER:	Damned British pig dog.
JUSTIN:	Are you sure you don't just imagine it?

(EVA takes drink to JUSTIN).

EVA:	Salude.

JUSTIN:	Oh thanks. But you haven't got one! You have to have one too you know.
EVA:	Of course! It is zee politesse. Adolphie, I bring for us zee Berchestgaden cocktails, ha ha ha.
HITLER:	Ha ha ha ha ha.
JUSTIN:	What's so funny?
HITLER:	You vill see... Juden.
JUSTIN:	I've told you before. I'm not Jewish. I'm Australian.
HITLER:	(*Suspiciously*) Zat may be. But you are still Juden.
JUSTIN:	Oh, bollocks.
HITLER:	Bollocks schmollocks. Soon you vill be as dust in zee dustpan. EVA!... where are you?
EVA:	I komm, mein lieblink. Und I bring for us zee Berchestgaden Cocktail, ha ha ha.
HITLER:	Ha ha ha. Zoon ve vill see who rules zee vorld.
JUSTIN:	Well I can tell you who it isn't. It isn't German National Socialism, that's for sure.
HITLER:	Pig dog! Juden! Take back your propagandas.
JUSTIN:	Look, Mr Hitler...
HITLER:	HERR Hitler!
JUSTIN:	Oh, OK. Look. Mr Herr Hitler...

(EVA approaches and hands HITLER a cocktail and holds one for herself).

HITLER:	Aha! We drink now to zee Fatherland. You vill join me.
JUSTIN:	You mean Germany? The reunited German Federal Republic?
HITLER:	Reunited? Vot means reunited.
JUSTIN:	Why, East and West Germany! The old Russian puppet and the Progressive democratic republic! United by the fall of the Berlin Wall! Don't they tell you anything down here?
HITLER:	You haf sense of humour, nein?

JUSTIN: Oh sure (*he raises his glass. HITLER and EVA do likewise.*)

(*The next three lines arre delivered imultaneously*)

JUSTIN: To Germany!
HITLER: To zee Fatherland!
EVA: Heil Hitler!

(*They all drink... JUSTIN quickly shows signs of being poisoned. HITLER and EVA watch his symptoms with professional interest*).

JUSTIN: (*Gasping for breath*) I've... got... to get my story... to the editor... (*he lurches offstage, then dies there very noisily*).

HITLER: Ach. So slow. Und only vun at a time.
EVA: But soon another komms.

(*Knock on the door*).

CHURCHILL: (*From offstage*) You there Adolph?
EVA: Aaaachhhh! Herr Churchill it is. Tuesday it must be.
HITLER: Zee Berchtesgaden Cocktail Eva. Ziss time ve get him.
EVA: As alvays I obey mein Fuhrer.
HITLER: Komm in Vinnie. Ve are expecting you.

(*CHURCHILL appears in the doorway, wearing a Homberg und smoking a cigar*).

CHURCHILL: Tuesday, Adolph... remember, your turn in the Brimstone Pit. Come on look lively... we haven't got all day.
EVA: But long enough, Herr Churchill, for... zee Berchtesgaden Cocktail... nein?
CHURCHILL: Not bloody likely.
HITLER: Ach. Perhaps after my immersion in zee bath of blood... yum yum yum!
EVA: Yummy yummy!

CHURCHILL; Don't kid yourselves. Today after the Brimstone Pit it's an afternoon in the Incredible Stifling Stench Room.

HITLER: Gott im Himmel. Not zee Stench Room!

CHURCHILL: Without a gas mask.

(Concerned reactions from HITLER and EVA).

HITLER: Vait. I negotiate.

CHURCHILL: Too late *(looks at watch)* I'm due for lunch with Ghandi in fifteen minutes. Get going!

(CHURCHILL waves and they are propelled OFF in stylized movements, mirrored in reverse by JUSTIN coming to life. CHURCHILL mops his brow).

JUSTIN: *(Rubbing his eyes in disbelief)* Mr Churchill! I mean, Sir Winston! Is it really you? What are you doing down here?

CHURCHILL: Sorry, lad, I can't stay. I've got an appointment in the other place.

JUSTIN: You mean – up there? What's it like – up there?

CHURCHILL: Bloody goat's milk and raw bloody vegetables with Ghandi for lunch again, I expect. Oh well – it could be worse *(He EXITS)*.

JUSTIN: What a scoop! Now. All I need's an angle. "Cocktails with Adolphe"? Nah *(as he wanders OFF)* "Churchill the Vegetarian," now that's a thought…

END

SKETCHES & MONOLOGUES

Writers who choose... or who are destined... to be poets, novelists or short story writers, are what might be called sole operators. Working alone, it's not until their current work is complete, or at least in its relatively advanced stages, that they are likely to seek the opinion of an editor, critic, or friend.

It's different for a drama writer, in that they very often need to see and hear what their work in progress looks and sounds like, in order to progress it. Snippets of dialogue and crucial dramatic turning points can sometimes show the way; and, incidentally, serve as useful acting exercises.

Frank Sutherland Davidson

Frank Sutherland Davidson

JARROD & PETE

Mates don't always agree with each other.

Cast: JARROD, a young man of 20ish,
       PETE, aged 20ish, his friend.

Setting: JARROD and PETE enter from different sides and meet centre stage.

JARROD: How's it goin' mate?
PETE: Not bad. Yerself?
JARROD: Can't complain.
PETE: Nah.
JARROD: 'Cept for the bloody mozzies.
PETE: Yeah. Somethink awful.
JARROD: Mind you. It's that time of year.
PETE: Yeah. S'pose so.
JARROD: Hey. Seen that sexy sheila lately?
PETE: Which one?
JARROD: You know. The one works in Woolies. Real sexy.
PETE: Ar... thought it was Coles.
JARROD: No, mate... Woolies.
PETE: Could be Aldi.
JARROD: Jeez mate... you're unobservant. She's a Woolies chick, definite.
PETE: Could be.
JARROD: No bloody could be, mate. She's definitely Woolies.
PETE: Not sure about that.
JARROD: You been talkin' to her?
PETE: Well...

JARROD:	You're a bloody dark horse. You've been chattin' her up... haven't you.
PETE:	Oh... Just saw her on the tram.
JARROD:	When?
PETE:	Well... today, as it happens.
JARROD:	An' you fronted her?
PETE:	Not really.
JARROD:	Wha'd'ya mean not really.
PETE:	She asked me... you know, on the tram... if I knew what time Coles opened.
JARROD:	Jeez! You're a mine of bloody information, aren't you.
PETE:	Well... I did say...
JARROD:	Spare me the bloody details. She fronts you, on the tram, and all you can do is tell her what time bloody Woolies opens
PETE:	Coles.
JARROD:	Bloody Coles then.
PETE:	That's how I know.
JARROD:	What? You know what?
PETE:	She works in Coles. Not Woolies.
JARROD:	Big deal.
PETE:	And... she clocks off at 5.30.
JARROD:	What? She told you that?
PETE:	No... I asked her.
JARROD:	Jeez. Now I've heard everything. She fronts you on the tram, and all you can find out is the time she knocks off.
PETE:	Well I needed to know.
JARROD:	(*Laughs*) Next you'll be tellin' me she asked you to pick her up when she knocks off.

PETE:	No... but she did say she'd be ready if I came round to the staff door at 5.30.
JARROD:	What?
PETE:	Yair... just before she got off at Coles I asked her to come to the disco with me tonight. But she's gotta go home and change first.
JARROD:	Go home? You know where she lives?
PETE:	Not yet. Will tonight, though.
JARROD:	Hey. Listen. Mate...
PETE:	Yep?
JARROD:	This disco you're goin' to...
PETE:	Yair?
JARROD:	Which one is it? (*pause*) Mind if I tag along?
PETE:	No way (*EXITS*).
JARROD:	Jeez that bloke's a dag (*EXITS*).

THE MORNING AFTER

Things may not work out the way we want.

Cast: MAVIS, a woman with definite views,
  AILEEN, her sympathetic neighbour.

Setting: Aileen's kitchen, where she is entertaining her neighbour Mavis to a cup of morning tea.

MAVIS: And I said to him, I'm not putting up with it, you can just get your own dinner if you're this late again.

AILEEN: What'd'e say?

MAVIS: Well. The hide of him, he said he'd rather get it himself anyway, than put up with it left in the oven to burn to a crisp.

AILEEN: He never.

MAVIS: His very words. Left in the oven to burn to a crisp, he said.

AILEEN: Ooh! What'd'you say?

MAVIS: That's when I said, if that's your attitude, I said, you can expect to get it yourself from now on, I'm on strike I said and see how that suits your arrangements, down at the pub every night of the week after work, maybe you can get one of your mates, I said, one of those mates of yours at the pub to peel your potatoes and put on your chops for you, see how you like that, I said.

AILEEN: Go on! You never!

MAVIS: I told 'im, straight. See how you like that, I said.

AILEEN: What'd'e say?

MAVIS: Well. He said something real funny.

AILEEN: Funny!

MAVIS: Oh not funny. Not, you know, something you'd laugh at. Far from it.

AILEEN:	Oh. Not funny.
MAVIS:	No. Peculiar, more like.
AILEEN:	Oh. Perculiar.
MAVIS:	Well. I have to say, I never expected it.
AILEEN:	No?
MAVIS:	No. After all, I've always been ladylike in my expressions, you'd agree with that wouldn't you Aileen?
AILEEN:	Oh yes. always.
MAVIS:	I don't hold with vulgarity.
AILEEN:	Oh no. Not even that time when you
MAVIS:	I was provoked.
AILEEN:	Oh yes. Prevoked.
MAVIS:	So. That's when I said to him, if that's your attitude, I said, the conversation's finished and I'm going to bed.
AILEEN:	What'd'e'say?
MAVIS:	Like I said. Something real peculiar.
AILEEN:	Perculiar, yes. What was it?
MAVIS:	Well. He said, Jeez you're pretty.
AILEEN:	Pretty what?
MAVIS:	Pretty. You know... attractive.
AILEEN:	Ooh er. Really? What'd'you say?
MAVIS:	I wasn't going to stand for that, I can tell you.
AILEEN:	No, why would you.
MAVIS:	Trying to butter me up.
AILEEN:	Oh, yes.
MAVIS:	That's when I said, the state you're in, I said, you wouldn't know pretty if you fell over it.
AILEEN:	Fell over it, yes.
MAVIS:	I won't tell you what he said next.

AILEEN:	No. Probably vulgar like, was it.
MAVIS:	Oh very forward. Especially considering the hour.
AILEEN:	Yes, and you on your way to bed.
MAVIS:	That's exactly what I told him. I'm on my way to bed I said.
AILEEN:	That told him.
MAVIS:	Yes. It did. It was what they call a tactical error.
AILEEN:	Really? What sort of an error?
MAVIS:	Tactical. Like what you do when you haven't thought out the ramifications of the situation.
AILEEN:	Oh. Yes. I wouldn't be bothered going to that much trouble.
MAVIS:	The trouble is, it took me by surprise.
AILEEN:	It did? What did?
MAVIS:	He moved.
AILEEN:	Oh? I didn't know he'd moved.
MAVIS:	I don't mean he moved. I mean – he moved on me.
AILEEN:	But you were on your way to bed, you said.
MAVIS:	Well, I thought, things could be worse... maybe I'll just go with the flow, if you know what I mean.
AILEEN:	Oh yes. The flow.
MAVIS:	So that's how we ended up... you know.
AILEEN:	Ooh... *(pause)* What happened to the chops?
MAVIS:	I heated them up. For his breakfast, like.
AILEEN:	Served him right. More tea?
MAVIS:	Just half a cup, thanks.

Frank Sutherland Davidson

LOTTO LOGIC

Sometimes you need advice & sometimes you don't!

Cast: BEN *self-important manipulator*
 CHARLIE *modest and thoughtful young guy*

Setting: BEN *and* CHARLIE *are standing in an open sapce.*
BEN: Hey! Charlie! Heard you won Lotto! Great to see you!
CHARLIE: Oh... hi, Ben.
BEN: Well, old buddy. I suppose you'll be wondering what to do with all the money *(laughs)* All your new-found wealth.
CHARLIE: Not really.
BEN: Got it all spent already, huh?
CHARLIE: It isn't paid out till they clear the ticket.
BEN: You know... it's times like this that you need a mate's advice.
CHARLIE: Yeah?
BEN: Someone in the know.
CHARLIE: You offering, are you, Ben?
BEN: Well, y'know, I do have a background in Finance.
CHARLIE: You do? How's that?
BEN: Oh, I did this course once... really puts you on top of it.
CHARLIE: So I suppose you've been managing your own finances pretty well then.
BEN: Oh yes. Got plenty of gilt edged investments, yeah.
CHARLIE: Go on! So you've got an independent income, then.
BEN: Workin' on it, mate.
CHARLIE: Sounds good.
BEN: *(Explaining)* So that's why I think that you should...
CHARLIE: *(In unison)* Hand over the money to you, to look after.

BEN: Hand over the money for me to look after.
BEN: That's the idea, mate.
CHARLIE: Y'know what?
BEN: Yeah?
CHARLIE: I think I've got the message.
BEN: Great, mate. When do we start?
CHARLIE: Oh, I'm not sure about that.
BEN: C'mon, mate, y'don't want to leave your new found wealth just lyin' about. Gotta put it to work, mate!
CHARLIE: Guess you're right.
BEN: So we can... I mean you can... sit back and watch it grow. Accumulate!
CHARLIE: Ar. Too bad I've already dealt with that problem.
BEN: What? What d'y mean?
CHARLIE: I've signed the winning ticket over to Lifeline.
BEN: What!!
CHARLIE: Yeah. I figured out there must be lots of people out there who need it more than I do.
BEN: You serious? You're not serious.
CHARLIE: Oh yes. Takes effect as soon as they verify the ticket and release the money.
BEN: (*Pause*) You stupid silly arsole.
CHARLIE: Hey, Ben... remember. Lifeline are always there if you need a hand. With your... financial arrangements (*EXITS L*).
BEN: What a selfish bloody moron (*EXITS R*).
END

Frank Sutherland Davidson

TWENTY YEARS AFTER

They went to the same school – but how have things changed?

Cast: JODIE, *a successful businesswoman,*
                   NOLA, *once was school captain.*

Setting: A corporate waiting room. ENTER NOLA R. *She looks about, then tentatively finds a seat.* ENTER JODIE L.

JODIE: Well! Hello! Nola! It is you, Nola, isn't it?

NOLA: (*Rising*) Oh yes. I wasn't sure I had the right place.

JODIE: You sure do! Amazing to see you again, after... how many years is it?

NOLA: Oh don't ask.

JODIE: (*Laughs*) Quite right. You know... I've always said, that the future... whatever it turns out to be... is more important than the past...

NOLA: Well... Jodie... let's not dwell too much on the past.

JODIE: No, indeed. Those days when you and I were at school together are something of a dim memory these days.

NOLA: Yes, I... I hope so.

JODIE: So... what brings you along today, Nola? I was absolutely amazed when my secretary told me that you'd rung and wanted to see me.

NOLA: Oh... thank you, yes. I was... well I was hoping that you might be able to give me the benefit of your advice... now that, you know, you've had such a... well... such a success in the business world.

JODIE: (*Laughs*) Hard work usually pays off, whatever field you're in.

NOLA: Yes, I remember when I was the captain of the hockey team at school...

JODIE:	Oh don't bring that up! I loathed playing hockey.
NOLA:	Yes, I remember, you usually had your head in a book or something.
JODIE:	Well I knew I'd have to make my own way in the world... I didn't have your advantages.
NOLA:	Well I suppose...
JODIE:	Of course everyone knew that you got to be school captain because your dad was such a local bigwig... big businessman, local mayor, and gave the school heaps of donations...
NOLA:	I...
JODIE:	While my mum was a single mother... pretty much frowned on in those days... with only a job in the pickle factory to keep us going, after my dad left.
NOLA;	Yes, I...
JODIE:	Still... it's made me what I am today.
NOLA:	Well...
JODIE:	Able to tread my own path, analyse situations, make corporate decisions, and lead a team... in business, not on the hockey field.
NOLA:	Oh yes. I heard you'd done well. Not like me.
JODIE:	Oh? Tell me... what have you done with your life... since we left school?
NOLA:	That's just it. I... you remember Brett... Brett Jarrow?
JODIE:	Of course! School glamour boy, captain of the footie team... your boyfriend, as I recall.
NOLA:	Yes... we were married after we left school.
JODIE:	Really! So you got your dream boat!
NOLA:	Not exactly.
JODIE:	Oh. Didn't turn out as expected?
NOLA:	No. But I do have a son...

JODIE: Well, that would be a consolation... wouldn't it?

NOLA: It's why I wanted to see you today.

JODIE: What does your son do?

NOLA: He's on welfare... at the moment.

JODIE: Qualifications?

NOLA: To tell you the truth... he's never really stuck at anything. So that's why I thought...

JODIE: You want me to see him? Give him an opening? Is that what you've come to see me about?

NOLA: If you would just consider...

JODIE: Look... Nola. We're a team of specialists here. We only take people occasionally, and only then when they have the qualifications we need. To be perfectly honest... we don't need an office boy. I'm sorry.

NOLA: Oh. Yes. I see.

JODIE: So that's it, I'm afraid.

NOLA: Well I mustn't keep you from... from your work.

JODIE: I do have a meeting in a few minutes.

NOLA: Goodbye then.

JODIE: If you want to call in again... you can always give my secretary a ring.

NOLA: Thank you (*she EXITS R*).

(*JODIE watches as she leaves and EXITS L*).

END

IN THE MOOD FOR MUSIC

There's probably a song for every event

Cast: ARTHUR, *a passing entertainer*
                 BASIL, *a forlorn lover.*

Setting: *A street or esplanade.*
ARTHUR: (*ENTERS singing*) Oh I do like to be beside the seaside...
BASIL: Oh put a sock in it.
ARTHUR: How dare you. I am an Entertainer.
BASIL: Well go and entertain somewhere else. Please.
ARTHUR: Not feeling well, are we? Liverish, perhaps? Too much of a good thing last night maybe?
BASIL: Mind your own business.
ARTHUR: I know what it's like.
BASIL: I doubt it.
ARTHUR: This is the Holiday Season. You're supposed to be happy and carefree...
BASIL: Tell that to my girlfriend.
ARTHUR: Oh ho! A lovers' quarrel!
BASIL: I suppose you've got a song about that too.
ARTHUR: Not yet but if you like I'll work on it (*sings*) Tea for two, and two for tea, me for you and you...
BASIL: Oh belt up will you.
ARTHUR: You know... if you took a more lighthearted approach to your problems...
BASIL: You mean triss around singing crap popular songs.
ARTHUR: Well, they don't have to be pop tunes. You could choose whatever takes your fancy. Music-wise.

BASIL: Yeah, and you can dredge up a song about some bastard that's taken my girlfriend out on his supercharged luxury cruiser for the day...

ARTHUR: And left you lonely and forlorn on the shore... I'm sure there'll be something in my repertoire.

BASIL: Don't try too hard. I'm not in the mood.

ARTHUR: Something upbeat.

BASIL: Up-beat... that's it!

ARTHUR: Look I'm not advocating violence…

BASIL: Why not? I know... I'll try it out on you. Look out!

(A great surge of music comes over the sound system, The Toreador's Song from "Carmen". Basil adopts a toreador stance and rushes at Arthur).

ARTHUR: *(Running off)* Help! Help!

BASIL: *(Stops in mid-rush)* Ahhhh. That's better. Good heavens. I think I can feel a song coming on.

(EXITS, singing "Managua Nicaragua is a beautiful spot; there's coffee and bananas and the temperature's hot...)

END

SALEYARD SAGA

A collison of cultures.

Cast: *NIGEL, a coutourier from Sydney*
WARREN, a local roustabout

Setting: *A country saleyard. WARREN is busy herding some (invisible) sheep. ENTER NIGEL.*

NIGEL: Oh my god. What is that appalling stink.

WARREN: Jeez, mate, you're lookin' a bit rare.

NIGEL: I must have had a blackout.

WARREN: No worries mate, you're just in time for the fat lamb auction.

NIGEL: Fat Lamb Auction??!!?? What's happened to my collection?

WARREN: Your collection? What of?

NIGEL: My new season's collection!

WARREN: Oh. Ya mean yer new season's lambs. Well, like...

NIGEL: No, you... you oaf. I mean my new season's hats.

WARREN: Shit, mate, ya don't need new hats here. Any old Akubra does fer the saleyards.

NIGEL: Saleyards??!!

WARREN: Yeah. We've just done the weathers.

NIGEL: I've got to find my consignment.

WARREN: Aw... probly still down at the goods yard.

NIGEL: Who is in charge?

WARREN: I am, mate.

NIGEL: I don't mean you. I mean, who is in charge?

WARREN: Like I just said, mate...

Frank Sutherland Davidson

NIGEL: I demand to see the manager.

WARREN: Well, that'll depend.

NIGEL: Immediately, thank you.

WARREN: Will that be the Elders Manager, or the Dalgety's Manager, or (*chuckles*) the Bank Manager, maybe? (*more chuckles*).

NIGEL: Just get me somebody in charge. Anybody. Before I faint from this hideous aroma.

WARREN: Mate, you work in the saleyards, you've just gotta get used to shit.

NIGEL: Oh my clients will never get over this. Nigel's Millinery Spring Collection having its showing in a saleyard. What is the name of this... this dump?

WARREN: Campfire Hills, mate. Tell that to yer fancy customers.

NIGEL: I'd rather die (*he faints*).

WARREN: (*After looking at the body*) Shit! I'll get the wheelbarra (*he wheels in the wheelbarrow*).

(*BLACKOUT. Scene changes to a bedroom in the Railway Hotel. NIGEL is unconscious on the bed.*)

WARREN: (*Fanning him with a copy of "Country Life"*) Come on mate. Stir yer shit.

NIGEL: (*Coming to*) Oh-oh-oh-oh-my head...

WARREN: Well ya hit yer head didn't ya, yer silly prick.

NIGEL: Where am I.

WARREN: The best pub in town, (*proudly*) The Railway!

NIGEL: The railway. Oh my god. I have to get my collection back to Sydney. When does the next train leave?

WARREN: Half an hour.

NIGEL: Can you get me there ?

WARREN: Sure thing mate, I'll just stick ya back in the wheelbarra an' we'll be down at the station in two shakes.

NIGEL: A wheelbarrow!? Oh... it doesn't matter... I'm past caring. Just as long as I can get my collection on board...

WARREN: Mate. There's just one thing.

NIGEL: Anything.

WARREN: Anything?

NIGEL: I'll do anything you want. Just... wheelbarrow me to the train in time.

WARREN: Jeez mate you're pretty keen to depart. But before ya do...

NIGEL: Oh what on earth is it you want? Money? A reference? My autograph?

WARREN: Well, mate. Them hats of yours.

NIGEL: Don't tell me you want one of them for your *(shudder)* your girlfriend.

WARREN: Shit no mate, she wouldn't be seen dead with one o' them on.

NIGEL: What??? You can't be serious.

WARREN: Well mate that's what she said, an' I make it a rule, never contradict a sheila *(aside)* that's if ya don't want a kick in the goolies.

NIGEL: Oh this is a nightmare

WARREN: Could be worse mate, Ya might have got yerself inta the crutchin' pen by mistake *(laughs)* Nah... like, this'll be no trouble fer ya.

NIGEL: Oh for god's sake get on with it. What do you want...

WARREN: Well mate I'm goin' to Sydney next week, see, fer the Mardi Garras, an' I'd like to complete me outfit with somethin' a bit special.

NIGEL: What! You want me to agree, for you to be seen, in public, in one of MY exclusive millinery creations...

WARREN: Yeah mate. But no worries... I've already got the frock...

NIGEL: Oh take the sodding lot. Just get me to the train. Now where is this ghastly wheelbarrow... (*limps off*).

WARREN: YES!!! (*making a gesture of triumph*).

END

CAFE ENCOUNTER

Sometimes you have to ask – what are friends for?

Cast: ROSEMARY, an overbearing socialite,
JUDITH, an acquaintance.

Setting: *A cafe in Double Bay, Sydney. JUDITH is seated at a table... ROSEMARY ENTERS.*

ROSEMARY: Why hello Judith.

JUDITH: Oh... Hello.

ROSEMARY: What a glorious morning. I'll join you if I may.

JUDITH: Why, of course.

ROSEMARY: I do hope you're keeping well.

JUDITH: Yes... these corona virus restrictions are so annoying... aren't they?

ROSEMARY: They certainly are. Have you ever heard of anything more ridiculous.

JUDITH: Never.

ROSEMARY: It's completely ruined my Thursday bridge afternoons.

JUDITH: Yes I heard you'd had to cancel them.

ROSEMARY: Oh? How did you manage to hear that?

JUDITH: I was talking to Janelle... as it happens.

ROSEMARY: Janelle? Janelle never comes to my Thursday afternoon bridge parties.

JUDITH: Oh I know.

ROSEMARY: So how would she know.

JUDITH: Yes she did mention that you'd never invited her.

ROSEMARY: Of course I haven't. Why would I.

JUDITH: That's one of the things she was wondering.

ROSEMARY: Well of course it's no secret that she drinks heavily and I make it a rule to serve only one glass of sherry, and that at the end of the afternoon.

JUDITH: Oh I don't think that's her perception of it.

ROSEMARY: Also she's a friend of that awful Magolski woman.

JUDITH: Oh you mean Marilyn Magolski.

ROSEMARY: Probably.

JUDITH: I don't think Marilyn plays bridge.

ROSEMARY Don't tell me you actually know her.

JUDITH: Oh yes. She's very active in our neighbourhood watch.

ROSEMARY: Sticking her nose into everyone's business.

JUDITH: Actually, no. That's not what neighbourhood watch is about.

ROSEMARY: Well it probably is, with her in it.

JUDITH: As a matter of fact, she was asking about you the other day, when I had coffee with her.

ROSEMARY: What! You had coffee with... what's her name...

JUDITH: Marilyn.

ROSEMARY: How could you.

JUDITH: Oh we get along quite well.

ROSEMARY: I can't imagine why. Coffee with Marilyn Mag-whatsername! I thought you had more social judgement.

JUDITH: (*Laughs*) Actually, I know quite a lot of people that you probably don't approve of.

ROSEMARY: That's impossible.

JUDITH: For instance... I'm having lunch today with Beverley Botham...

ROSEMARY: What! That two-faced...

JUDITH: I know she voted against you in the last Community Club elections...

(ROSEMARY blows her nose loudly).

JUDITH: But, you know, there are always two sides to every opinion.

ROSEMARY: Not to mine.

JUDITH: Perhaps if you'd been prepared to listen...

ROSEMARY: I don't listen to people of that type.

JUDITH: What type?

ROSEMARY: That type.

JUDITH: Yes, I see. That does make it clearer.

ROSEMARY: Judith dear, there are some people in this world that simply aren't worth knowing and if I were you, I'd choose the people I mix with a little more carefully.

JUDITH: Rosemary, I do know what you mean. One really does have to be careful.

ROSEMARY: Particularly to be avoided are people of... you know, that type... whose sole aim is to impose themselves on others.

JUDITH: Oh very valuable advice, Rosemary. Most valuable.

ROSEMARY: Yes. Do try to take it to heart...

JUDITH: I'll especially remember it while I'm having lunch.

ROSEMARY: Glad to hear it. Are you having lunch here?

JUDITH: Yes, as a matter of fact. I've got two friends joining me...

ROSEMARY: Oh. What a pity I can't join you...

JUDITH: I'm not sure that you'd want to.

ROSEMARY: Yes I know it's a bit shoddy but the food is acceptable... so I'm told.

JUDITH: One of my favourite places, in fact.

ROSEMARY: Entirely suitable... if you're lunching with... that Beverley Botham *(looking at her watch)*.

JUDITH: Yes, and the other lunch guest.

ROSEMARY: Another friend?

JUDITH: Yes... Marilyn Magolski.

ROSEMARY: It's been so lovely to catch up but I'm afraid I must be going.

JUDITH: Always delightful to see you Rosemary.

ROSEMARY: Absolutely. I do hope we can catch up... another time.

JUDITH: I shall so look forward to it (*looks OFF*) Oh! Here they come now. Marilyn and Beverley.

ROSEMARY: Goodbye (*EXITs*).

END

COMING HOME TODAY

A monologue.

Cast: MAN, *a sufferer*

Setting: *A bare stage.*

Well. Today's the day. So they've told me.

Now here's the question though. Do I believe them.

Hah! Let's look at both sides of it.

One. That big woman with the veil. Maaaa... tron. She said I was going today. But she said I have to wait for "the escort".

That's a laugh. Ha ha.

Two. That doctor bloke. What did he say?

Can't remember.

Oh yeah... *(mimicking)* "Well, old son, we've done all we can for you here.. Time to move on." Thanks a lot.

What am I doing here anyway?

Oh I know what they tried to say.

That I was "a danger to myself and others."

Bloody pricks.

You don't know the half of it.

What I did to that guy... he deserved it.

I don't want to think about it.

Leave it. Let it go. Let... it... go!

So will I get out of here today? If I do -- what then.

109

(*Suddenly*) Maybe they'll give me back the key to my flat.

I can get a lift over there. Get a hitch maybe.

It's a busy road. Someone will stop.

Not like that time when I stood there in the rain.

When was that? I don't remember. I feel... sick.

I don't remember. Why did she do that? I loved her. Still do. Like I said... always will.

It couldn't have been her fault.

I'll never understand why he was there. What was he doing there? How did he come? How did he get in? She wouldn't have let him in.

Mongrel... Bastard.

I saw what he was doing. I knew what he wanted. You don't have to be told these things. Hit him with the baseball bat. Floored him... real good. Rotten prick. Blood... blood everywhere.

Couldn't stop her screaming. Tried to. I knew there'd be trouble. Not her fault... why was she undressed? Had to cover her up – put the pillow over her, tried to stop the screams. After that... nothing. They said I'd been there for two days. Just sat there. Holding her...

"Come with us, Jim," they said. Put this thing on me... this... jacket. Couldn't move. Straight-jacket. Funny word (*maybe a laugh, tailing off...*)

Then I woke up here. Now... they tell me it's over. Maybe I'll be getting out. Going somewhere else.

But it's not over. I know what I have to do. Get a lift. Back to the flat.

"Get yourself cleaned up, Jim, you're going

somewhere today." Had a shower. I was allowed to shave myself. I'll be ready when I get home.

Straight to the bathroom. Go to where I left her, on the bed.

Yes. I want to lie down where I left her. Just two slashes... one here, one here.

Hope they come soon. Soon be peak hour. Get that lift. Coming home today. Today's the day.

END

Frank Sutherland Davidson

PRISON

A monologue.

Cast: MAN, *a convicted murderer.*

Setting: *A bare stage.*

The night we're talking about.

The reason I'm in here.

He came at me with a knife. Under the streetlight.

That's why I hit him with every bit of strength I had. I knew he was unconscious.

But I didn't think he was dead.

I had to protect myself! He meant to kill me. I could see it in his eyes.

I never provoked him...

That Prosecutor, at the trial... he's evil. He made it seem like it was my idea to kill him.

How could that be? I didn't know anything until I saw the flash of his knife...

The way he came on!

I only had seconds to try to avoid the knife, the pain, whatever he was going to do to me.

But I was too quick for him.

Oh yes.

Just as he would have stabbed me, I hit him, fair and square.

Right in the face. Yes, with the iron bar.

Where did I get it from?

It was right there, wasn't it. I saw it... leaning against the wall.

It's not true that I went up to the Junction looking for trouble.

I've got enough trouble in my life.

Why would I go looking for more.

It's no different in here.

There's always someone who wants to have a go at you.

Makes no difference if you're locked up or out in the yard.

I've always had to protect myself.

Always had to...

Ever since that time...

I was just a kid.

Filthy old perv.

"Come in here, boy, I've got something to show you."

Oh yeah.

Tried to get away... Ugh.

Still makes me feel sick just to think of it.

Oh yeah. Years trying to forget that.

You never can... not completely.

I don't trust people.

Always on the lookout.

Keep yourself to yourself... that's what I say.

Why did that old perv have a knife? When he took me?

"If you tell anyone about this I'll come after you and I'll cut your balls off".

That's what he said.

As though I hadn't had enough.

But I wasn't going to cry... not any more.

I'd been through the pain... I was somewhere on the other side of it.

The old perv didn't know it... how would he... but that night, that night he did that to me, in my mind, I killed him.

Right there. On the spot.

I didn't feel anything any more.

I just stood there... even stopped shaking.

"I won't tell nobody, mister," I said.

He let me go, then.

"Make sure you don't," he said, "or I'll do it. I'll come after you and I'll do it."

As soon as I felt his knife go off me, I went. Like the wind.

This is the best part. The only good part. Whenever it comes back – I see him lying there dead.

I'm not even sure how I kill him.

Sometimes it's different...

Sometimes I grab the knife off him and stab him through the heart.

Sometimes I smash his head in, like with a hammer, or something.

But always, I get away and he's lying there, crumpled up, dead.

I don't understand though... why he always comes back.

At least in here, locked up... there's only yourself to cope with.

Except during exercises, or in the showers.

But I know enough now.

I think they're scared of me, in here.

Good thing.

I'd like to forget... maybe, some day, I'll be able to.

Who knows.

Until then... there'll always be someone... someone who brings it back.

Like that guy under the street light... how he looked at me.

It wasn't my fault he had a knife.

Now, they tell me, he's dead; and it's my fault.

At least... that's what the jury people said. But they weren't there, were they?

I'm the one that has to live with it.

Nothing takes it away... you have to go on living with it.

For as long as you can.

I'll be in here for a long time.

Here.

In this cell.

In this lonely place.

But the loneliest place?

Right here (he taps his chest)

END

Frank Sutherland Davidson

PLAYS FOR CHILD AUDIENCES

These scripts originated from interest based classes I ran while working at Sydney Teachers' College with students preparing to be Primary and Infants teachers.

Growing from theme discussions, improvisation sessions, scripting exercises and finally production for presentation, the scripts were played by the students in classrooms for children in nearby schools.

I particularly want to thank all the students who chose to join these classes at the College, contributed to the final scripts and took part in the performances. I also want to thank the students in the Drama Department of the University of New England who polished a performance of one, "The Mystery of the Black Moon", as a class exercise at the University.

Frank Sutherland Davidson

THE MAGICIAN'S CLOAK
A play for children aged 6-8 years

Cast: MAGICIAN, *a good ruler of his kingdom,*
VIPERELLA, *a witch,*
ZEPHERINA, *the Magician's daughter,*
THE PRINCE, *a good prince,*
TREE 1, *a prisoner of Viparella,*
TREE 2, *a prisoner of Viparella,*
ROCK-FAIRY, *a good fairy*

Setting: *A castle wall. C, a rock and a pile of seaweed. L and R are two TREES. A loud clap of thunder, followed by a triumphant, continuous cackle from VIPERELLA. As if propelled, the MAGICIAN appears over the castle wall and is hurled C. As he gradually recovers, VIPERELLA's cackle subsides.*

MAGICIAN: *(Holding his head)* Oh...oh... what happened? I feel as though I've been hit by a great bolt of lightning. Did you hear it? If I could just think what happened... now ...*(begins walking around)* What was I doing....Oh! My daughter, Zepherina, and I were ...ZEPHERINA!! Where is she? I remember now! We were out... walking around our kingdom... we do that every morning, to see that all our people are happy and the animals safe... and just as we went back inside the castle there was this terrible thunder... we must have been thrown right out of our own house! Because the next thing I remember is waking up here. And where is Zepherina! *(he calls)* ZEPHERINA! She doesn't answer... *(cackling from the castle)*... that sound... there's only one person in the whole world who makes that noise... the Witch! Viperella! *(more cackling, gradually mounting through his speech until VIPERELLA enters)* And she's in the castle! It was she who made that thunder! *(with determination)* She must be stopped before she puts an evil spell on all of us. She will be stopped! My power is greater

119

than hers, because whoever wears my magic cloak... (*discovers his cloak is missing*) My cloak. My magic cloak. It's gone... (*running towards castle*)... surely this can't mean...

(*ENTER VIPERELLA*)

VIPERELLA: YESSSSSSSSS!!!!!!! At last, I've done it! Done it! Tricked the Magician! Thrown him out, and captured his silly little daughter. For years I've wanted to get my hands on this kingdom of his. The animals grow so fat here... there are sure to be lots of plump slimy things I can use to put into my cauldron... for a witch's brew! And all the foolish people who live here... from now on, all my slaves. I'll make them give me their finest cloth for my bed and their fattest sheep for my table. And they'll all have to bow down to me... twice a day! Oh, I'm going to be so comfortable in this castle. And now for the greatest prize of all (*holds up the MAGICIAN's cloak*) The Magician's cloak! Whoever wears this cloak, rules this kingdom! And so... (*putting on cloak... as she does so, thunder in the background*)... the kingdom is mine. Everything is in my power. The earth itself obeys my commands.

MAGICIAN: So it was you! How dare you bring your evil powers into my kingdom! Creep into my castle and...

VIPERELLA: Your castle? Is it your castle now? I don't see your name on the door. It is mine! And... I have put a spell on your daughter that will last while ever I command here... she shall lie lifeless in my castle for a hundred years and nothing will wake her unless I undo the magic I have made (*cackling*) I have your daughter and your cloak and your castle and your kingdom. I am all-powerful and magnificent, and I shall rule here forever and ever! And now... go! Before I turn you into a stone.

MAGICIAN: Oh what am I going to do! If only she hadn't stolen my cloak... but my daughter! Lifeless while ever she commands! I can't let her get away with that (*to VIPERELLA*) If I go... will you grant me one favour? Give me back my daughter. She is young and beautiful, and one day she will be a Princess. You dare not keep her. Undo your magic... bring her back to life... and release her from your wicked spell.

VIPERELLA: (*Laughing scornfully*) Release her! Do you think I'm mad? You dare ask me for favours? I don't do favours for fools. You have no power to ask anything of me.

MAGICIAN: Please... my daughter. I'll do anything to have her back by my side. Just remember. Magic doesn't always turn out the way you want it. Are you sure you know how to use the Magician's cloak?

VIPERELLA: (*Aside*) H'm! I don't know how to use it, but I'm not going to let him know that, the old bag of bones (*to MAGICIAN*) So... you'll do anything, will you, if I bring your daughter back to life.

MAGICIAN: Anything.

VIPERELLA: And what do you think you can offer me, when already I wear your cloak and sit in your castle and rule your kingdom?

MAGICIAN: (*Aside*) It's true. I haven't anything. But that's because she has stolen everything, and put her horrible spell on Zepherina! I haven't anything to bargain with. Unless... (*to VIPERELLA, rhetorically*)... What have I to offer?

VIPERELLA: (*Preening*) Well... (*sarcastically*) what have you?

MAGICIAN: (*Aside*) My magic cloak... she doesn't realise that my cloak can't be used for wicked magic... only for good. There's just a chance...

VIPERELLA: I wait no longer. Decide!

MAGICIAN: All right. I'll make a bargain with you. You have stolen my cloak... but, if you bring my daughter back to life, I'll give up all claims to it! You will then be its rightful owner... and can use it for whatever you want. It will be the Magician's cloak no more, my kingdom will be yours, and Zepherina and I will go far, far away, where you will never hear of us again.

VIPEELLA: (*Aside*) And if the Magician's Cloak is the Magician's cloak no longer, I can use it to turn them both to stone before they have gone three steps... and then, there will be no-one to dispute my claim to the castle and the kingdom and all within it! (*to MAGICIAN*) It is agreed. I will grant you that... but first... renounce your Cloak!

MAGICIAN: I will do it.
By the seven stars of wonder
The Magician's Cloak is mine no longer.
Let Viperella wear it newly
And be it hers who wears it truly!

(*As the MAGICIAN's spell concludes there is the sound of a soft gong*)

VIPERELLA: Mine! Mine! The cloak is mine! Am I not magnificent? Have ever before the stars shone on such beauty as is now mine! Bow down before me, trees. Look on me, clouds, and tell me as you pass, whether ever before on earth there has been anyone as beautiful as Viperella. My brilliance surpasses the sun... all magnificence is mine and (*screaming*) I SHALL DO JUST WHAT I LIKE FROM NOW ON.

MAGICIAN: But first, you ust keep your promise. You must bring Zepherina back to life.

VIPERELLA: Oh, I'll do that all right (*carelessly*):
Break the bonds of sleep asunder,
Zepherina wake in wonder...
and much good may it do you.

ZEPHERINA: (*Appearing on the castle*) Father!

MAGICIAN: Zepherina! At last you're free... come down, we must leave our home, we have a long way to travel and we must start our journey.

ZEPHERINA: Oh Father... what has happened? I long to be by your side... but... oh Father... I can't move!

VIPERELLA: Stay! Wretched little girl.

MAGICIAN: What! You promised! We made a bargain.

VIPERELLA: Fool! Never trust a witch's bargain. I have kept my promise. All I said was that I would bring her back to life. And this I have done. Now she is my SLAVE! And you, Magician, go on your journey alone. I was going to turn you into stone... but a stone has no feelings. It would be too good for you. Go now before I turn you into a worm and step on you. Begone!

MAGICIAN: Evil woman, you will pay for this.

VIPERELLA: (*Going on to castle wall*) Quickly, before I destroy both you and your daughter (*grabs ZEPHERINA roughly*)

ZEPHERINA: Help! Help!

MAGICIAN: By the powers...

VIPERELLA: Powers? You have no powers! You just gave then all to me... remember? Get out of my domain! (*scream of triumph, leading into song*).

(*Chorus*)
I'm a witch, I'm a witch,
I'm a nasty old witch,
And now I rule this great big land;
I hate everybody and I hate everything,
You must do my command

(*Verse 1*)
I mix up a brew of slugs and snails,
And snakes, and worms from the well... ooh, delicious...
I stir it all up in my cauldrom black
And it makes a terrible smell.

(*Repeat Chorus*)

(*Verse 2*)
I have a cloak of beautiful cloth
It's almost as beautiful as me,
And if I cast one of my wicked spells
I could turn you into a tree.

(*Repeat Chorus*)

Come here, you wretched slave! Fetch me the

slimiest slugs and the grizzliest grubs from my most dismal dungeons. I need them for my cauldron to mix a witch's brew. Away with you, you scrawny little weakling. I hate the sight of your pale pretty face and your skinny little body and your dainty little feet. Begone! Go! Before I change my mind!

(VIPERELLA chases ZEPHERINA into the castle).

MAGICIAN: Zepherina is the witch's slave! Oh how could I have been so stupid. But it won't be forever. You know... bad things come when we least expect them. But good things can happen just as suddenly. Especially if you're... cheerful... and... keep smiling... *(he is nearly in tears)*... and hoping... and your friends are there to help you... oh, if only I wasn't alone... *(VIPERELLA is heard cackling from the castle)* What am I thinking of! This is no time to be sorry for myself. Viperella has stolen my kingdom and my cloak. And she has made my daughter a slave. There must be something I can do. Even without my magic cloak *(the MAGICIAN begins to stride up and down)* And whatever it is, I will think and think and think *(he trips over the seaweed)* until I know what it is. Now. If I walk up and down, over here where she can't see me, perhaps it will come to me. Witches are short-sighted, you know. As long as I don't go too near the castle she won't know I'm here *(trips a second time)* That's funny... there's something that keeps running through my mind... like a spell... only it's not a spell. More like a rhyme:

Tree trunks... rock face... seaweed and quince
Viperella's day is done when I find the...

(Trips a third time... there is groan from under the seaweed and a hand shows. It is the PRINCE)

PRINCE: *(Dazed, still under the seaweed)* Where am I? Oh... my head...

(The MAGICIAN backs away while the seaweed begins to move and the PRINCE gets to his feet. He is wearing a long seaweed-covered cloak).

MAGICIAN: What is this? More of Viperella's evil magic? I must be very careful what I say.

(The PRINCE suddenly sees the MAGICIAN and draws his sword).

MAGICIAN: Why do you draw your sword on an unarmed man?

PRINCE: Who are you sir.

MAGICIAN: Who are you, sir.

PRINCE: *(Looking at his clothes, brushing off seaweed)* I am a prince. Well... I was until a little while ago. I am travelling a very long way... because I am on a quest to do battle with evil wherever I find it.

MAGICIAN: And what have you found to do battle with, so far?

PRINCE: Oh, I'm sorry *(puts up his sword)* You must think I'm very rude. The fact is... I've been used to defending myself. Two dragons; and a wicked knight who had his people all chained up in his dungeons. I fought him and won... but now that I have proved my valour, my next task is to defeat evil without force of arms. I suppose that's why I'm here... *(looking around)* What place is this?

MAGICIAN: But how did you get here? You weren't here this morning.

PRINCE: I don't know! There was a great clap of thunder... and that's the last I remember.

MAGICIAN: *(To himself)* Thunder? ... seaweed... Q for quince.. "Viperella's day is done ... when I find ... THE PRINCE!" *(going to the PRINCE and clasping his hand)* Sir! You are very welcome. Fear me not... I can do you no harm. Tell me... does the name Viperella mean anything to you?

PRINCE: Do you mean that this is Viperella's castle? At last! I've been looking for that evil witch for many weeks *(hand on sword)* Are you a servant of hers?

MAGICIAN: By the magic moonbeams, no! In fact I am, or was, her greatest enemy.

PRINCE: Sir... forgive me for asking these questions. But you see, I must be sure who my friends are. And if you are... or were... Viperella's greatest enemy... then I know who you are. You are the Magician who rules the Country Next-to-the-Sea; and you are in very great danger.

MAGICIAN: I'm afraid your warning is too late. She came this morning... surprised Zepherina and me... now she sits in my castle, wearing my magic cloak, and she has made my daughter her slave, to help her make her evil witch's brew.

PRINCE: Then this is it! My next task. Sir... I am Prince Quentin, and my mission is to defeat Viperella and make her sorry for her bad deeds. Don't be downhearted any longer. You and I together will find a way to rescue your daughter and regain your magic cloak.

MAGICIAN: But how? I have already tried... and she has tricked me with her evil witch's tricks. All my power lies in the cloak.

PRINCE: You don't always need magic. There must be a way without using the cloak. Suppose we sit down, and you tell me how to get into the castle *(they sit down on the rock)*.

MAGICIAN: Well, we can't go to the front... she would see us straight away. But even if we could get round to the back door without being noticed... she would still see us coming.

PRINCE: So we can't go together. But if one of us could attract her attention, and keep her talking for long enough...

MAGICIAN: While the other one...

PRINCE: Crept round to the back door...

MAGICIAN: Slipped inside the castle...

PRINCE: And while she wasn't looking, helped your daughter Zepherina to escape... then we could all sit down here and plan how to win back the cloak!

MAGICIAN:	It will be very dangerous for all of us... but we must try it (*he rises*).
PRINCE:	(*Rising*) There is no other way.

(*VIPERLLA appears on the castle. She carries a telescope which she puts to her eye*).

MAGICIAN:	Quick! Hide!

(*They hide behind the rock*)

VIPERELLA:	(*Looking through the wrong end of the telescope*) Curses! I can't find anything to eat in his abominable castle. Not a fat sheep in sight... where does that Magician keep them all? (*she comes down from the castle*) And I'm so thirsty... I can hardly wait for a nice long drink of witch's brew... with a crackly, crawly cockroach to crunch (*returning to the castle*) Where is that stupid girl? If she doesn't hurry up with my ingredients I'm going to chop her up and eat her for lunch (*calling*) Where are you slave? Bring me a mirror! (*throws cloak about her in grand manner*) I must look at myself, I am so majestically beautiful and evil.

(*ZEPHERINA hurries in with mirror*)

ZEPHERINA	Here is my mirror.
VIPERELLA:	(*Very angry*) Your mirror? MY MIRROR! (*she snatches mirror, thrusts telescope at ZEPHERINA and begins to look at herself in mirror*) Well? What are you waiting for?
ZEPHERINA:	Is there anything else? Because I would like to look through the telescope... to see if I can catch a last glimpse of my father.
VIPERELLA:	(*Furious*) You have already looked your last on him and if you don't get back to the dungeons immediately and gather more slugs I will put you in my cauldron as well (*ZEPHERINA hesitates*) Begone! Or I'll turn you into a tree! (*ZEPHERINA goes, leaving the telescope, VIPERELLA gives a cackle*) Oh, I won't be turning her into a tree just yet. She's far too useful.
MAGICIAN:	Now's our chance. But we'll have to be very careful... she could turn us both into trees at any moment. I'll go this way and you go that... and the guidance of the seven stars go with you!

PRINCE: Right!

(They begin their separate moves, halting whenever VIPERELLA is turned towards them)

VIPERELLA: *(Looking in the mirror)* Yes, I'm certainly a handsome picture. If only this mirror could talk... to tell me how beautiful I am. Well of course! *(laughs)* Now that I have the Magician's cloak, I can make any magic I like! Now... *(she prepares for a spell)*

MAGICIAN: Oh Evil One! I must speak to you.

VIPERELLA: *(Looking through telescope, again through the wrong end)* You there! How dare you enter my domain without my permission! Who are you?

MAGICIAN: *(Aside)* She doesn't recognize me! *(disguising his voice)* I am a traveller... who seeks the beautiful Viperella, ruler of this kingdom.

VIPERELLA: *(Simpering)* Well... I'll just see if she's at home *(she puts her head inside the castle... aside)* What am I saying? *(aloud, grandly)* I am she. What want you with her... er, me?

MAGICIAN: *(As before)* I have heard that you possess great powers of magic. I have come to see how great these powers may be.

VIPERELLA: Perfectly true. I have the most magnificent cloak in the world... given to me by the Magician who used to rule here before I... er... came along *(shows off cloak)* With this cloak I can do any magic you might care to see... if I feel in the mood for it.

MAGICIAN: And can you show me your magic? So that I may spread your fame abroad?

VIPERELLA: Well, that depends. I'll have to see if I can think of something nasty enough to do *(cackle)* Of course! I've got a useless slave here... a silly, scrawny little thing, no good for anything, can't tell a slug from a cockroach. Just wait out there and I'll call her up and turn her into a tree for you.

MAGICIAN: *(Gasps)* Turn her into a tree? *(in his own voice, thunderously)* By the seven stars... (He runs towards the castle).

VIPERELLA: The seven stars? It's YOU! You stupid, meddling old fool... (*meanwhile, the PRINCE has entered the castle from the back and now appears behind VIPERELLA, leading ZEPHERINA by the hand*)... this is the last time you trick me.

PRINCE: Jump, Zepherina, jump!

(*The PRINCE jumps first, then turns to catch ZEPHERINA. She follows but before her feet touch the ground the witch has commenced her spell; ZEPHERINA gradually becomes lifeless as the spell progresses*)

VIPERELLA: All that is evil!
The girl I awoke
Now with the power of the witch's cloak,
Down, down, down and be still...
You! Sleep forever! For that is my will.

(*The PRINCE lays ZEPHERINA on the ground. There is a clap of thunder and while VIPERELLA screams her spell, she gestures at the PRINCE and the MAGICIAN, who run for cover to the rock*) Spies! Traitors! I will skin you alive and boil your bones! Trespassers to my domain! Thieves! I will be revenged on you! My cauldron. I will make the wickedest witch's brew that ever a wicked witch brewed... and when I catch them they will be tortured and tormented by toads, bitten by barnacles and cracked and crunched by crocodiles. Away! To the dungeons! For I have work to do... to make an evil brew... a grisly, gruesome stew... to give me power, within my tower, to lure those meddling two!

(*VIPERELLA EXITS screaming; the MAGICIAN and the PRINCE are in hiding behind the rock. Silence and after a pause, there is the sound of a flute or recorder playing a sweet melody. Gradually the branches of the TREES begin to move in time and through the rustling of leaves words become distinguished as the TREES sing*):

Don't be frightened
We can see you
Trees are moving
We're alive.

>   Don't be frightened
>   We can help you
>   Evil witches
>   Never thrive.
>   Viperella
>   Was our mistress,
>   We refused to
>   Do her will;
>   For a hundred years
>   Or more now
>   We have been here
>   Standing still.
>
>   *(As the music dies way the Trees resume their previous positions L and R)*

MAGICIAN:	They're spirits! Spirits that the witch has locked in the trees
PRINCE:	They say they've been there for over a hundred years!
MAGICIAN:	And I didn't even know *(goes over to each TREE)* These trees have been here ever since I have ruled over this kingdom. I suppose I must have walked past them every morning. And all the time, in each tree, the witch had her prisoner... oh, Prince Quentin,... despite my wisdom and my magic arts, I have been ignorant and blind. But now I am more sure than ever that we can defeat the witch and rescue Zephyrina.
PRINCE:	Why this sudden change of heart?
MAGICIAN:	Didn't you notice? Viperella used my cloak to put my daughter under a spell.
PRINCE:	I noticed. I have never seen any Princess, in all the countries I have visited, who looked more beautiful than Zephyrina... awake or asleep.
MAGICIAN:	And when the spell was completed... what happened?
PRINCE:	There she lay... as still as death ad as cold as stone *(he gazes at her)*.

MAGICIAN: Yes, yes, but she'll be all right when we get the cloak back again. Didn't you see what else happened.

PRINCE: No... (*he shakes his head, still looking sorrowfully at ZEPHERINA*).

MAGICIAN: Think again.

PRINCE: I can't think at all. My heart is too full. I have the most wonderful feeling... that somehow... when all this is finished... Zephyrina is going to be my bride.

MAGICIAN: Yes. The rhyme told me that...when we first met, here, by the rock... (*he quotes*) "Tree trunks, rock face, seaweed and quince... Viperella's day is done... for I've found... Zephyrina's prince!"

PRINCE: You knew? And you think, do you, that we'll be able to get the cloak back, and break the spell?

MAGICIAN: Sure of it. You see, when the spell came down on Zephyrina... it came up from someone else (*he gestures*)

PRINCE: The trees! (*the TREES sway, bow and rustle their leaves in acknowledgement*).

MAGICIAN: You see... whenever she uses the Magician's Cloak to do a bad deed... Viperella can't help doing a good one as well! That's how the trees are able to move now. And when the spell is broken altogether, I'll make them both into people... and they shall be Zephyrina's faithful attendants (*the TREES give small joyful jumps, and shaking their branches, sing*):

Our lady is to be a Princess
We will serve her long and well;
Arms, not branches, will we have then;
Ding, dong, ding, the wedding bell.

We will do for you, Magician,
Anything you need us to;
All to serve the cause of battle
Banish witch and witch's brew.

All together, Prince, Magician,
Storm with us the castle wall;
Follow us, we go before you

Find a way to make you tall...
Find a way to make you, make you,
Make you, make you, make you tall.

(Having been moving slowly towards the castle, the TREES now stop)

PRINCE: Well, this'll be the first time I've ever gone into battle with trees instead of soldiers, but... if we follow behind them up to the castle the witch will never know we're there. It's a disguise better than a whole troop of soldiers.

MAGICIAN: Yes. But we still need help to get over the wall. All the magic isn't done yet.

PRINCE: What do you mean?

MAGICIAN: *(To himself)* "...tree trunks...rock face...rock face... *(suddenly)* Of course! *(to PRINCE)* The rhyme said the rock had a face too. And if it has a face it must be a fairy. Fairies can make themselves into any shape... this rock is the last part of the rhyme.

PRINCE: *(Quoting)* "Find a way to make you tall."

MAGICIAN: *(Still thinking)* Mm?

PRINCE: *(Laughing)* It isn't magic... I suppose that's why I thought of it.

MAGICIAN: Ah... but you're a soldier, and a soldier has to think well in battle. And we have another life to save here, besides our own.

PRINCE: I know *(gestures to ZEPHERINA)* Should I bring her down here, out of the way of the battle?

ROCK: No *(PRINCE jumps away)*.

PRINCE: What was that!

ROCK: Leave her where she is.

PRINCE: I don't understand. Is it another spirit?

MAGICIAN: No. It's a fairy. It was she who gave me the rhyme, and she will help us to defeat Viperella once and for all.

PRINCE: Couldn't you just ask her what to do?

MAGICIAN: (*Laughs*) Oh she wouldn't tell us that easily. No, we must work it out for ourselves. And I think you are going to be the one to think of it.

PRINCE: Well... I heard what those trees said... "Find a way to make you tall". But there's nothing hre we could use... except this rock. And it's in the wrong place.

ROCK: Push me, hide near me, climb the wall softly.

(*VIPERELLA appears on the castle, carrying her cauldron*).

MAGICIAN: Quick! Do what she says.

(*They both hide behind the rock and start to push it towards the castle*).

VIPERELLA: This is the thickest, most gruesome brew I've ever brewed. Just wait till it boils, the smell will be deliciously vile and horrid. It's bound to make enough evil magic to fix those two trespassers for good. After I've caught them I think I'll put them down in the dungeons to start with, and after a week or two of that I'll hang them by their heels in the tower. When they've got used to being my slaves, I'll make them start a vegetable garden for me. Fortunately I've got a good supply of seeds... poison ivy, deadly nightshade, stinging nettles, and a varied selection of summer thistles (*displays her bag of seeds*) They can grow all over this prize I've got sleeping out in front (*cackle*) She won't look so beautiful then! (*picks up telescope*) What are those trees doing? (*MAGICIAN and PRINCE freeze*) You! How dare you take this liberty, Who gave you permission to approach my castle?

TREE 1: We come to pay homage to the all-powerful ruler of our kingdom.

TREE 2 Whose home is in this castle.

VIPERELLA: (*Pleased*) So... you recognize my greatness, and come to bring me that which I deserve.

TREES: (*Together*) We do, we do... (*bowing*).

VIPERELLA: Naturally I am the greatest beauty in the land.

TREES: *(Continually bowing during this exchange)* Oh no, oh no.

VIPERELLA: The most supreme, the cleverest, the wisest.

TREES: Untrue, untrue.

VIPERELLA: The most majestic... *(double take)*... What? Untrue!? Beware my anger! I will have no spies and traitors here!

TREES: *(Triumphantly)* Too late, too late!

(Meanwhile, having reached the castle, the MAGICIAN crouches behind the ROCK while the PRINCE climbs on top of it and suddenly sprints over the wall behind VIPERELLA; he takes hold of the cloak and removes it from her shoulders; she recovers in time to grab the bottom of the cloak and they struggle, facing each other)

PRINCE: I can't move!

VIPERELLA: Traitors to the witch's cloak
Spying strangers, foolish trees,
Hands of ice enfold and grip you!
Stand forever solid... FREEZE!

(At the conclusion of the spell there is a loud discordant burst of noise, thunder, crashes from within the castle, and interspersed with this the sound of a gong; after awhile the gong's rhythm pattern dominates and it is joined by the recorder, triangles etc until their melody gradually defeats the cacophony. Both VIPERELLA and the PRINCE stand frozen but on sound cues, the ROCK undergoes a transformation and becomes a FAIRY. She removes the headdresses from the TREES, assisted by the MAGICIAN; they are now people and turn in circles on the spot, silently expressing joy on their release. Suddenly the sound stops. The TREES become still. The PRINCE and VIPERELLA are still frozen; the MAGICIAN and the ROCK-FAIRY are the only ones who can talk and move.)

ROCK-FAIRY: It is done. The cloak is yours again, and with it, the kingdom.

MAGICIAN: Who are you?

ROCK-FAIRY: I have many names, and many faces. But in your kingdom... I shall be known as the Rock-Fairy and

	I shall always be here to watch over your daughter, She shall be as wise as she is beautiful and one day she shall rule here in your place.
MAGICIAN:	When will that be?
ROCK-FAIRY:	Not yet. But when your time here is finished, and you begin your journey amongst the seven stars... then shall she and the Prince take your place... and she shall wear your magic cloak, so that together they shall rule wisely and well.
MAGICIAN:	All thanks and honour to you, Rock-Fairy.
ROCK-FAIRY:	Peace and happiness to you, Magician, and to your kingdom.
MAGICIAN:	And Viperella... what shall we do with hr?
ROCK-FAIRY:	She must be made to undo the mischief she has done here. (*she goes to the back of the castle and appears between VIPERELLA and the PRINCE*).

Wicked woman, Viperella,
All your plans have come to nought.
Evil deeds have been defeated,
By your cauldron you are caught.

Now undo your wicked doings,
Make our Princess come to life;
Then release the Prince from bondage,
He will take her for his wife;

You must suffer good for evil,
Witches all must pay the price;
Tortured you will be until you
Make your Cauldron something nice!

(*The ROCK-FAIRY takes the cloak from the hands of the PRINCE and VIPERELLA and hands it to the MAGICIAN; she then releases the PRINCE, who comes out of the spell and swiftly jumps down from the castle to kneel by the side of ZEPHERINA; the TREES go to stand by her feet. Finally, VIPERELLA comes out of the spell and is very uncomfortable*)

PRINCE:	Zephyrina!

TREES: Our mistress! We wait for your command.

VIPERELLA: Toads and toenails! What has happened? Where is my cloak? Villains! Imposters! (*she sees ROCK-FAIRY*) YOU!

ROCK-FAIRY: Yes, Viperella. You surely didn't think I'd let you get away with your wickedness again. This time you pay even more dearly. You know what you have to do. About it!

(ROCK-FAIRY gestures. VIPERELLA is propelled over castle wall, landing in a heap just as the MAGICIAN did at the beginning. She scrambles to her feet, trying to remember her various spells and losing them as she careers madly about, finally coming to rest in the spot initially occupied by the ROCK).

VIPERELLA: Ooh, I'll be revenged on the whole pack of you! (*she is racked by torments*) Ooh! Ow! (*etc until she finally appeals to the audience*) What do I have to do? (*the actress must sort out responses and, perform the following: invest the MAGICIAN with his cloak; release ZEPHERINA from her sleep; and finally, using her bag of seeds, which contains cordial crystals, turn her cauldron into orange juice*)

Tableau for final song and procession. (Reprise "Our lady is to be a Princess").

Actors break out beakers and invite audience to taste the cauldron; the Princess ladles out orange juice while the others distribute it.

ABOVE THE SKY & BEHIND THE STARS

A play for primary school children.

Cast: MOTHER, *a harassed single parent*,
KELLY, *her youngest child, about 6*,
LIZ, *her second child, about 8*,
LEO, *her eldest, about 10*,
LINDA, *a good witch*,
NELLY-PELLY, *a bad witch (doubles later as Mrs Pelly)*,
CALIFRAX, *an automated space monitoring system*,
SPACE SCANNER 1 }
SPACE SCANNER 2 } *space monitors*
SPACE SCANNER 3 }
SPIDER-WITCH, *another bad witch*,
CREEPY, *Spider-Witch's 1st servant*,
CRAWLY, *Spider Witch's 2nd servant*,
WHISTLER }
DRUMMER } *Music Makers*
CHIMER }

Setting: *A screen as backdrop. A raised platform upstage for the Music Makers; otherwise, the playing area is an open space.*

(*Voices of the three children OFF*)

But we didn't mean it Mum, I didn't do anything... What's it matter anyway?

MOTHER: (*OFF*) I've told you kids before and I'll tell you again, you stay out of trouble or I'll wallop you, good and proper. Now in there you go and here's something to be going on with... (*sounds of whacking, reactions after each. ENTER the three CHILDREN*).

KELLY: Ow. That hurt!

LIZ: I'll pay you back Mum. Just you wait.

LEO: Aw, come on. At least we'll be by ourselves in here.

LIZ: Why does Mum pick on us so much?

LEO: Well, maybe we shouldn't have tipped out her wardrobe and built a cubby house in it.

KELLY: I only wanted to do my toenails with her nail polish.

LIZ: Well you shouldn't have spilt it on the floor. Anyway, you're too young.

KELLY: I am not.

LEO: Aw, come on. Don't start a fight. Not when we've got to stop in here the whole afternoon.

LIZ: Yes, with nothing to do.

KELLY: We could tell stories.

LEO: Yeah, ghost stories.

KELLY: Oh, no, Leo!

LIZ: Ooh, yes Leo! Tell us a ghost story!

KELLY: No!

LIZ: Baby!

LEO: Aw, come on.

LIZ: Go on Leo. Kelly can cover her ears. Can't you, Kelly.

KELLY: You're mean and I hate you and I'm not your friend.

LIZ: Big deal!

LEO: Aw, come on Kelly. I won't make it scary, I promise.

KELLY: Liz always makes fun of me because I get frightened when you tell ghost stories, Leo.

LEO: Well, what about if I make Liz promise. Liz, you promise not to laugh at Kelly?

LIZ: Who cares.

LEO: Go on, Liz.

LIZ: Oh all right.

LEO: Say it.

LIZ: Why? I just said it.

LEO: You know what I mean. Say you won't laugh when Kelly gets frightened.

KELLY:	But you promised it wouldn't be scary
LIZ:	Baby!
KELLY:	(*Starting to whimper*) Oh!
LEO:	I know! I'll tell a monster story instead. Once upon a time there were three children.
LIZ:	Just like us.
LEO:	Yeah. Their mother was a witch. A real scary witch, with big red eyes and a wart on her nose.
KELLY:	What's a wart?
LEO:	And one day, she made them go inside her broom cupboard where she kept all her magic brooms.
LIZ:	Just 'cos they'd been naughty.
LEO:	Yeah, 'cause they tipped out her wardrobe (*he starts to laugh*).
LIZ:	And made a cubbyhouse in it! (*she laughs too*).
KELLY:	And put polish on their toenails! Ooh, go on, Leo!
LEO:	And there they were, in this broom cupboard, see, waiting in there, when all of a sudden there was this big, big noise.
LIZ:	Go on!
KELLY:	What was it, Leo!
LIZ:	It was the monster, silly.
LEO:	It was the monster, and it was just outside the door, breathing smoke. And fumes.
KELLY:	And it made a big noise.
LIZ:	How do you know?
KELLY:	'Cause I heard it.
LIZ:	When!
LEO:	Aw, come on. This is my story. You didn't hear it.
KELLY:	Did so.
LIZ:	Can't you keep quiet, Kelly...

(They start bickering; LEO tries to shout over them; suddenly outside the door, a loud BANG).

LIZ: What was that!

KELLY: It's the monster! *(she runs to hide between LIZ and LEO).*

LEO: I'm going to have a look *(he EXITS and calls out)* It's a box! *(he ENTERS holding the box)* They've just left it at the door.

KELLY: Leo! Leo! Maybe the monster sent it.

LEO: What?

KELLY: And the monster did send it, and it's got a spell on it, and when you open it the monster comes out, swoosh, and eats you up...

LIZ: It's not locked.

KELLY: Don't open it!

LEO: We could just have a look inside.

LIZ: To see what it is.

KELLY: No!

LIZ: *(Kindly)* Don't worry Kelly. There isn't really a monster, you know that. And we'll only have a little peek.

LEO: Ok then. Let's have a look.

(LEO holds the lid open and LIZ takes out the STONE and holds it up. Simultaneously, the SOUNDS begin and LINDA appears upstage but remains unseen by the children).

KELLY: Ohhhh

LEO: Wow!

LIZ: I... I can't move!

LINDA: This stone is magic. It belongs
To the Music Makers.
Without it, their songs
Have lost their meaning.

You'll hear them try to play,

	But without the magic Their music has gone away.
	Who stole it doesn't matter, But who finds it and returns it They will be remembered And for them the music waits to play.
LIZ:	There's someone here!
LINDA:	Someone from above the sky, behind the stars! For that is where, once upon a time, a witch called Nelly-Pelly stole this Stone from the Music Makers! But now... Liz and her brother and sister will need my help... as you shall see... sooner than I expected...
	(ENTER NELLY-PELLY)
NELLY-PELLY:	(*Sings*) I'm the evil Nelly-Pelly I'm nasty and I'm smelly And I live in bins and other people's drawers
	I don't bother much to dress up And I love a place to mess up So I'll smash your plates and dirty up your floors.
	You won't even know I'm coming 'Cos I'm singing and I'm humming Yodel-aidy, I'll be going through your bin;
	And I'm coming at the double 'Cos I love it when there's Trouble... I'm the evil Nelly-Pelly and I'll WIN!
LINDA:	Come on, I'll look after you. We can't stay here.
LEO:	Where are we going?
LINDA:	Above the sky and behind the stars.
LIZ:	How?
LINDA:	Hold onto my cloak.
NELLY-PELLY:	(*To LINDA*) HAAAAAAA!! It's you again! You've got the Stone that makes music. This time you won't get away with it. I'll find it if it's the last thing I do.
LEO:	It will be.

NELLY-PELLY: Who said that! Where's the cheeky brat!

LINDA: Hold on! *(she collects the CHILDREN).*

NELLY-PELLY: *(Laughs)* No matter how far ahead you are I'll catch you... sooner or later.

LINDA: But you'll never be able to use the Stone... it isn't yours... you stole it *(LINDA with the CHILDREN whirls OFF UL).*

NELLY-PELLY: Don't think you can get away from me with your fancy flying, anybody can do that, and look out everybody because here goes!

(As NELLY-PELLY whirls unsteadily around the area, the setting changes to SPACE with CALIFRAX centre stage UC).

CALIFRAX: Califrax, the Radar Emergency Service Satellite, is registering a disturbance on Earth. We must find out what is happening there and why we have been alerted. Scanners! Everybody to your posts. When trouble starts we must warn the Galaxy. Our job is to keep the disturbance under control. Scanners, what can you tell us?

(SCANNERS 1, 2 and 3 ENTER performing the RADAR DANCE during which the CHILDREN are whirled in).

CALIFRAX: So you are the cause of this disturbance. And yet not entirely, for our Scanner are warning us that the main force of the attack is still on its way. Well... what do you have to tell us about yourselves?

LEO: Er... ah... we... er...

LIZ: Shut up Leo. Don't say anything.

KELLY: Are you the Queen?

CALIFRAX: In a way. I have to see that everything runs properly here. We have to see that no-one gets hurt. And you have got something with you that, if it gets into the wrong hands, could hurt us all.

LEO: Ah... er...

LIZ: What are you going to do with us?

CALIFRAX:	That will depend on you. And on what happens to the Stone.
LIZ:	They want it too! It must be very valuable.
CALIFRAX:	You'll see the Music Makers try to play, But without the magic Stone, Their music has gone away.
	Who stole it doesn't matter, But who finds it will be remembered And for them the music waits to play.
	(The SPACE SCANNERS become agitated, signalling an unwelcome approach).
CALIFFRAX:	I have told you all I can. Give me the Stone, before it is too late, and we can see that it reaches the Music Makers.
LIZ:	But what can happen?
CALIFRAX:	We don't know. Something is coming from your Planet. The Scanners know it is bad, but...
KELLY:	I know who it is. The scary one.
CALIFRAX:	You have seen her?
KELLY:	Yes! She's really ugly. And she's got a terrible voice. Ugh! *(she covers her ears).*
CALFFRAX:	It must be Nelly-Pelly! If she gets the Stone, no-one will hear anything but the ugly sounds she makes. The Music Makers will never be heard again. Quickly! The Stone!
	(As LIZ is getting it out, there is a terrible noise from NELLY-PELLY arriving UR. The SCANNERS intercept her but she shrugs them off and goes careering around the space).
NELLY-PELLY:	Lovely place you've got here. Oops! *(she falls over)* Who did that? *(she goes about as though looking for the culprit).* Well! I said I'd catch up sooner or later, and it looks as though it's sooner. You'd better give me that Stone, because I want it. Get out of the way *(she pushes the SCANNERS).* I know it's here, but who's got it? *(she catches KELLY, who screams).*

KELLY: Let me go, you ugly old witch!

(*KELLY bites NELLY-PELLY'S hand*).

NELLY-PELLY: Argh! I'm going to eat you alive for that.

LIZ: (*To CALIFRAX*) Here! Quick!

(*LIZ tries to throw the STONE to CALIFRAX but NELLY-PELLY catches it*).

(*NELLY-PELLY laughs, and as she does so and mimes speech, cacophony is emitted by the instruments. The CHILDREN cover their ears and run about. The effect on the SCANNERS and on CALIFRAX is lethal, they break down and are sinking fast when LINDA whirls into the middle of the melee, NELLY-PELLY is knocked over and LIZ manages to take the STONE from her grasp. The SPACE characters are whirled away, followed by the CHILDREN*).

LINDA: We've been too quick for you again, Nelly-Pelly. You'll have to be cleverer than this, if you want to keep the Stone. But you'll never get it away from us now. It's on its way back to the Music Makers.

NELLY-PELLY: I've got friends, you know. You might get a big surprise. Just you watch.

(*NELLY-PELLY tries to whirl and falls over. LINDA laughs and whirls off UL. Change of scene to SPIDER-WITCH'S web. ENTER two SPIDERS, CREEPY and CRAWLY; they perform a slow motion spider dance and introduce SPIDER-WITCH who arranges herself languidly UC The SPIDERS continue their rhythm*).

SPIDER-WITCH: (*Clicking her fingers*) Come here.

(*The SPIDERS approach*).

SPIDER-WITCH: Anything in the web this morning?

CREEPY: No more than usual, Your Repellance. Just a few flies. But they're very thin.

CRAWLY: I saw some fat ones.

CREEPY: (*Aside*) Shh! We want to keep some for ourselves.

SPIDER-WITCH: Bring me the fattest. I feel like a good meal.

CREEPY: (*Yawns*) I'm tired. Wouldn't you rather wait till after lunch?

SPIDER-WITCH: Move it, Twinkletoes. I haven't had breakfast yet.

CREEPY: Oh, yes, Your Repellance.

SPIDER-WITCH: Wait! There's something coming. Something BIG. I can feel it. More than one of them in fact. They're in the Web now (*her mouth waters*) Mmmmmmmmm! This is going to be worth waiting for. Stand by to collect.

(The CHILDREN are whirled in UR).

LEO: Pfh! What is this stuff.

LIZ: It's like cobwebs.

LEO: It's dark in here. Where are we?

KELLY: I hope it isn't a monster.

LIZ: Stay close, Kelly, I don't want to lose you and I don't want to lose this Stone.

LEO: Just don't talk about the Stone till we find out where we are.

(The CHILDREN explore. As they go past, the two SPIDERS uncover their faces and follow).

SPIDER-WITCH: Seize them!

(The SPIDERS wind them about with web thread).

SPIDER-WITCH: OooH! Lovely! Ooh, I don't know which one to eat first.

LEO: You stay away from us, you… you…

KELLY: You monster!

SPIDER-WITCH: Don't you call me a monster, you little human being. You're in my Web and from now on you do as I say.

LIZ: Who are you anyway.

SPIDER-WITCH: I am the Spider-Witch. I spin the Web that catches all the lazy and careless people. And sometimes those that are just plain unlucky. They're the ones I enjoy most.

LEO: Surely you don't ...eat...people?

SPIDER-WITCH: (*Laughs*) Oh, I do, I do! Not straight away though.

SPIDERS: (*Laughing*) Oh no, not straight away.

SPIDER-WITCH: BE QUIET! *(to the CHILDREN)* No, not straight away. First, I sting you. And once I do, you'll never be able to leave here.

LEO: Wh-why not?

SPIDER-WITCH: Because in my sting is the poison of which you humans can never have enough.

LIZ: We don't want any of it.

SPIDER-WITCH: You don't now. But once you've had it... then even if you do get away from here, you will always come back because you will always want more. And it's nice here. You'll like it. We have fun. DON'T WE?

SPIDERS: Oh yes... we do.

SPIDER-WITCH: Before I inject, show them your Spider Dance.

CREEPY: Oh just get on with it.

CRAWLY: (*Yawning*) We've done it once today already.

SPIDER-WITCH: You see? Here everyone does exactly as they want.

LIZ: If that's so... then let us go.

SPIDER-WITCH: So. You're going to make trouble. You're the one I'll inject first.

(SPIDER-WITCH gets out a big hypodermic syringe. The CHIDREN struggle against the web thread. The SPIDERS become very excited and move around the CHILDREN).

LIZ: You let me go, you old witch. You'll be sorry if you don't.

(SPIDER-WITCH plunges in the needle but the injection is not successful).

SPIDER-WITCH: What! It's broken. What have you got in your pocket.

KELLY: Oh Liz! The Stone! The Stone!

(Loud bumps and tearing noises OFF. Cries and confusion from the SPIDERS. ENTER NELLY-PELLY, bound up in web thread).

NELLY-PELLY: Hello, everybody... Oh I'm glad I got here safely.

SPIDER-WITCH: You horrible clumsy thing, you've ruined my Web. You're going to have to pay for this.

NELLY-PELLY: Oh what's the matter with you.

SPIDER-WITCH: I'll show you a thing or two!

(She chases NELLY-PELLY with the syringe).

NELLY-PELLY: Stop! Let's talk this over. We can work together –

SPIDER-WITCH: Grab her you fools... don't just stand there –

NELLY-PELLY: A fine friend you turned out to be.

SPIDER-WITCH: What have you ever done for me.

NELLY-PELLY: Well, probably not much. But I can do something now.

SPIDER-WITCH: What?

NELLY-PELLY: See these horrible little human persons who have absolutely ruined your beautiful Web?

SPIDER-WITCH: What are you talking about, you big bundle of rags. You ruined my Web!

NELLY-PELLY: Well I can tell you how to fix it. You won't have to lift a finger.

SPIDER-WITCH: *(Furious)* I haven't got as finger to lift. Only humans and things like that have got fingers.

NELLY=PELLY: They've got a magic Stone with them. Get it off them, give it to me, and I'll see that your Web is fixed in a twixt.

SPIDER-WITCH: First... you take back that bit about lifting a finger.

NELLY-PELLY: Oh all right. You won't have to lift one of your legs.

SPIDER-WITCH: That's more like it. Now. What was all this business.

NELLY-PELLY: The STONE! Who's got it? Eh?

LIZ: You leave us alone.

LEO:	If we give you the Stone can you help us get out of here?
LIZ:	No, Leo!
NELLY-PELLY:	That's for sure. Just hand it over and you'll be out in a twixt.
KELLY:	I don't believe her.
LIZ:	Neither do I.
LEO:	And you've got to help us escape from here.
NELLY-PELLY:	Oh I'll do that all right.
LEO:	How can we be sure?
NELLY-PELLY:	Why, I always help my friends.
SPIDER-WITCH:	Hold it. I thought you were supposed to be my friend.
NELLY-PELLY:	Well of course I am, I am.
SPIDER-WITCH:	Then what are you doing giving away my breakfast. I want the lot of them.
NELLY-PELLY:	Of course you do. *(To LEO)* Just hand it over and we'll work out the details later.
LEO:	No!
NELLY-PELLY:	Let her have the others and I'll take you with me.
LEO:	What! Why, you... You're not getting the Stone off Liz while there's a breath left in my body.
NELLY-PELLY:	So! It's Liz who's got the Stone. Now we know. That one. Get her.
SPIDER-WITCH:	I knew she was a trouble maker. Look, she broke my hypodermic.
NELLY-PELLY:	We'll make her pay for it.
	(NELLY-PELLY holds LIZ while SPIDER-WITCH feels in her pocket. LIZ screams, KELLY cries).
SPIDER-WITCH:	Got it!
NELLY-PELLY:	Hand it over.

SPIDER-WITCH: Don't forget my Web.

(SPIDER-WITCH gives the Stone to NELLY-PELLY. There is a blast of cacophony as NELLY-PELLY brings out a transistor radio from under her clothes. The SPIDERS are galvanised into a disco movement).

CREEPY: Oh wow!

CRAWLY: The greatest!

SPIDERS: *(Together)* Spin! Spin! Spin the Web Spin! Spin! Spin the Web *(repeated).*

(As they dance LINDA whirls in UR. She clears the space and the SPIDERS are blown OFF. NELLY-PELLY is knocked over).

LINDA: Quickly! Tie her up.

(Using the Web threads, the CHILDREN tie up NELLY-PELLY).

NELLY-PELLY: What are you doing?

LINDA: I think we might leave you here. Amongst your friends.

NELLY-PELLY: Oh no! Not here!

LEO: Why not! You were going to leave Liz and Kelly here.

LIZ: Is the Stone all right? It saved my life.

LINDA: Yes, it's all right. It can never be destroyed. But it can be used for evil if it is in the wrong hands.

KELLY: Is that why you look after it?

LINDA: Yes. I have to see that it is returned to the Music Makers.

LEO: Couldn't you just take it back?

LINDA: That would be the simplest thing, wouldn't it. But it's not the right thing.

LIZ: What do you mean?

LINDA: I will tell you. Unless people... such as you... are prepared to learn how to look after the magic

	secrets, there will always be the bad ones... like Nelly-Pelly here... who will want to use them badly. And you three have been chosen to help me return the Stone.
LEO:	You mean this is a reward? Why? Because Mum smacked us?
LINDA:	Yes, if you like. And when you go back to your Mother, you might be able to help her too.
LIZ:	Gee! Imagine telling Mum anything.
LINDA:	Your Mother needs your help. She is very busy trying to keep you together as a family and she is not good at explaining what she means.
KELLY:	I love my Mum and I'm going to help.
LINDA:	Yes, you will all help more because of what has happened today. But we still have work to do. Hold onto my cloak, because now we must try to reach... the Music Makers.
NELLY-PELLY:	Here! You can't just leave me... take me with you, I'll be *(shudder)* I'll be good! Don't leave me out here in space...
	(But LINDA and the CHILDREN have whirled off UL and NELLY-PELLY stumbles OFF after them).
	(ENTER the Music Makers, WHISTLER, DRUMMER and CHIMER trying to play but making only discord).
WHISTLER:	We have had a message from the Califrax Radar Emergency Satellite. There is an evil spirit loose in Space. We have to be prepared for an unwelcome visitor.
DRUMMER:	It was bad when we took in the Nelly-Pelly who came unannounced.
CHIMER:	Well we have learned from that. We know that even our magic Stone is not safe from evil witches.
WHISTLER:	But will we ever see the Stone again!
DRUMMER:	It will come back to us, for there are still people on Earth who listen for our music and hear it silently.

CHIMER: We will see them here one day... and for them the music waits to play.

WHISTLER: But before that, we will have other visitors.

DRUMMER: It it certain they will come?

WHISTLER: They will be here soon.

CHIMER: They are coming now. I can feel their music. Oh I wish we didn't have to play it.

WHISTLER: We can't escape that. But remember that help is not far behind and our Stone is on its way home.

DRUMMER: They are getting closer and closer... soon I won't be able to keep their music back...

CHIMER: I can no longer... I must play it...

(MUSIC MAKERS commence discordant playing and a wail song. SPIDER-WITCH and SPIDERS arrive).

SPIDER-WITCH: Mmmmmmm! Very tasty looking creatures. This is just the place for a new Web. Well, what are you waiting for? Start spinning.

(The SPIDERS commence spinning. The MUSIC MAKERS are drawn together into the Web).

SPIDER-WITCH: And now... breakfast.

(SPIDER-WITCH gets out her hypodermic syringe. As this happens, the note of the MUSIC MAKERS changes and they look eagerly UR anticipating the arrival of LINDA).

SPIDER-WITCH: Bring me... that one *(pointing at WHISTLER)*.

CREEPY: Yes... your Repellance!

CRAWLY: Certainly, your Repellance!

CREEPY: Will there be enough for us?

SPIDER-WITCH: Oh there must be plenty of these around.

(They have brought WHISTLER before SPIDER-WITCH).

WHISTLER: You can destroy us if that is your will. But you cannot destroy our magic or our music.

SPIDER-WITCH: What do I care about your magic. All I want is a good meal.

(The SPIDERS make slurping noises).

WHISTLER: If you sting us... you will be punished.

SPIDER-WITCH: Ha ha. You must be joking. I don't intend to let anyone punish me.

CREEPY: Oh can't you hurry up, your Repellance!

CRAWLY: We're starving!

SPIDER-WITCH: Prepare to inject.

(SPIDER-WITCH raises hypodermic but as she does so, the CHILDREN arrive one by one followed by LINDA and as they arrive the SPIDER-WITCH and the SPIDERS become progressively frozen and the Web holding the MUSIC MAKERS is unwound and harmonious sounds commence).

WHISTLER: You have saved us... and returned our music. And the magic Stone!

LINDA: Yes. My friends here have learned its value.

WHISTLER: And what do your friends suggest that we do with the Spider-Witch and her Spiders?

LINDA: Leo? Liz? Kelly?

LEO: Aw... gee... I dunno...

LIZ: Come on Leo. You always have the ideas.

DRUMMER: They cannot remain here.

CHIMER: But where can they go, and how?

LEO: I know where they should go. Back to Nelly-Pelly. Then they can fight it out together.

WHISTLER: A good idea!

LINDA: We can all help to prepare them for their journey.

(They fold all the legs of the three SPIDERS so that they are made into balls. In pairs, the MUSIC MAKERS and the CHILDREN prepare to push the SPIDERS off into Space).

LINDA: Now! *(she whirls centre stage; the SPIDERS are rolled OFF UL).*

LIZ:	And now... to return what is yours.
	(LIZ returns the Stone to WHISTLER. The CHILREN are whirled OFF).
WHISTLER:	Will you stay with us?
LINDA:	No. I must return with them.
WHISTLER:	Must you? Califrax and the Scanners will see that they travel safely back to Earth.
LINDA:	There is some help they will need there.
WHISTLER:	Then... farewell...
DRUMIMER:	Till next time we meet...
CHIMER:	Above the sky...
ALL:	And beyond the stars!
	(LINDA whirls OFF. The MUSIC MAKERS make a circuit of the space before they EXIT).
MOTHER:	*(OFF)* Leo! Liz! Kelly! You can come out now. Leo! Liz! Kelly! Answer me! *(she ENTERS)* Kelly? Liz? Leo? How could they have got out... I thought I locked the door! *(worried)* Kelly! Where are you?
	(KELLY ENTERS).
KELLY:	Here I am Mum. What can I do to help you.
MOTHER:	Where were you?
KELLY:	I've been here all the time.
MOTHER:	But where are the others?
	(LEO ENTERS).
LEO:	I'm here Mum. What can we do for you?
MOTHER:	But... but...
	(LIZ ENTERS).
LIZ:	Hello Mum. Are you ready to let us out now? We'd like to tidy up your wardrobe and put all your things back.
MOTHER:	I don't understand... I thought...

LIZ: What did you think. Mum?

MOTHER: Oh... nothing. It doesn't matter. Did you really mean it when you said you wanted to tidy up?

CHILDREN: Oh yes Mum... Yes Mum... Yeah

MOTHER: Well... (*she puts her arms around them*) I'll tell you what you can do for me. A friend of mine called Mrs Pelly is coming in for a cup of tea. Maybe you could...

KELLY: Did you say... Mrs -- Pelly? Mum?

MOTHER: Mrs Pelly, yes.

LIZ: Are you sure she's a friend of yours?

MOTHER: Eh? Of course I'm sure. I met her down at Bingo last night..

MRS PELLY: (*OFF*) Yoo hoo!

MOTHER: Oh here she is now.

(*ENTER NELLY-PELLY... but groomed and well-dressed*).

MRS PELLY: Lovely place you have here Oops! (she trips)

MOTHER: Oh it is nice of you to say that Mrs Pelly. I do try to keep it nice but there's just so much to do... looking after the children...

MRS PELLY: Oh? You have children? (*she peers around short-sightedly*).

MOTHER: Yes... Leo, Liz, Kelly, say hello to Mrs Pelly.

CHILDREN: Hello.

MRS PELLY: Well... as long as they can be seen and not heard.

MOTHER: Come along and have a cup of tea Mrs Pelly. It's good of you to come... I get so lonely here with only the children for company...

(*EXIT MOTHER and MRS PELLY*).

LEO: Was that...

LIZ: Yes.

LEO: What are we going to do?

LIZ:	What can we do! She's going to come here and pretend to be Mum's friend...
LEO:	And that's not the worst.
LIZ:	What do you mean?
LEO:	Where did we send the Spider-Witch?
KELLY:	Back to Nelly-Pelly.
LEO:	Back to Nelly-Pelly. So they can fight it out together.
LIZ:	Here.
LEO:	Here.
LIZ:	Oh.
KELLY:	What are we going to do?
LIZ:	Couldn't we try to tell Mum?
LEO:	Do you really think she would understand?
LIZ:	No.
LEO:	All we can try to do is try to let her see what Nelly-Pelly is really like.
KELLY:	Or find a new friend.
LIINDA:	(*OFF*) Yoo hoo!
LIZ:	What was that?
LEO:	Someone else is coming.
LIZ:	Is it the Spider-Witch?

(*The CHILDREN face upstage as though preparing to meet an enemy. ENTER LINDA*).

KELLY:	Oh! (*she runs to LINDA and hugs her*).
LIZ:	Oh!
LEO:	Boy, is it good to see you.
LINDA:	So you know who I am
KELLY:	Of course we do.
LIZ:	But... there's someone else here too.

LINDA:	I know. Why do you think I came?
	(They all laugh together).
LIZ:	*(Calling)* Oh Mum! Mum!
MOTHER:	*(OFF)* Yes, dear.
LIZ:	Is Mrs Pelly still here?
MOTHER:	Yes of course. What do you want?
LIZ:	Oh nothing... except there's someone here we'd like you to meet.
KELLY:	She's a friend of ours.
LINDA:	Come on.
	(They all EXIT together).
	END

THE MYSTERY OF THE BLACK MOON

A play for children aged 8 and over.
Can be staged with or without the suggested theatrical effects.

Cast: ASTRO (m), a leading Space Explorer from Earth,
NAUT (f), also a Space Explorer from Earth,
THE STORYTELLER (f), a Space dweller,
THE WARRIOR (m), King of "Arthura the Brilliant,"
LUNARIA, a space ruler
PLANETORIA, another space ruler
THE PRESIDENT OF SPACE
THE IMPRISONED QUEEN

Setting: *When the audience enters, this is what they see.*

Three low small platforms mark the triangular acting area: UC, DR, DL.

On each platform stands a costume mask, later to be inhabited by three actors but at present each is exhibited as though in a Space museum.

There can be slight, surreal suggestions of SPACE elsewhere.

Spotlights on the three platforms. In the centre of the acting area the BLACK MOON. Special spots on the BLACK MOON.

In shape and construction the moon can be dodecahedron but there must be provision for one actor to enter and exit freely at the back of it.

Visible on top of the moon should be the Space Crown which is later brought down when required. Sound and Lighting should already be setting the atmosphere.

Lights fade to Blackout. Theme music. Moon spots up.

The BLACK MOON slowly begins to descend to centre stage.

Soundtrack segue into fragments of spaceship sounds and

inter-corn crew messages.

Over these can be heard the voices of ASTRO and NAUT, still on the soundtrack but leading into their dialogue as the spaceship sounds climax and are replaced by surreal sounds which can accompany and punctuate the action from time to time during the play.

When ASTRO and NAUT enter they are whirled into the acting area and circle the BLACK MOON as though in orbit around it, each also turning on his/her own axis.

(ENTER NAUT).

ASTRO: (*Off*): Space control!!! Space control!!! Space control!!!

NAUT: Astro! Astro!! Where's the space rope?

ASTRO: (*Off*): Gone!

NAUT: Where?

(ENTER ASTRO).

ASTRO: It tore out of my hands!

NAUT: (*Frightened*): Oh!

ASTRO: We're completely out of touch with control.

(During the next speeches they both gradually ease to slow motion).

NAUT: There's a gravity pull.

ASTRO: (*Pointing at the BLACK MOON*): It's coming from there!

NAUT: Try to work back!

ASTRO: (*His gesture frozen*): I can't. It's a magnetic field!

NAUT: I'm frightened ... (*gravity also begins to affect her*).

ASTRO: (*Urgently*) Don't get too close to it!

(ASTRO and NAUT are now turning slowly at L and R of the area respectively).

NAUT: (*Suddenly stopping*) This moon's not on our astrochart.

	No one from Earth's ever been here before! Just think... maybe they'll name it after us! (*She starts to turn as before*).
ASTRO:	(*Still turning*). That's if we ever get away from here again! Ohhh ... (*he spins down towards the Moon, collapsing near it, L, a simulated landing*).
NAUT:	(*Shouting after him*): Look on the bright side Astro. We're landing on an undiscovered moon! (To audience) Or maybe its just a bit of space waste after all. Oh dear... I wish I were at home in bed... dreaming ... (*she spins down and lands on the Moon, R*).

(*THE STORYTELLER appears from behind the Moon. She runs to each Astronaut, inspects them, and is satisfied. Then she confronts the audience*).

STORYTELLER:	This is how it was. These are 'The Two' who came to the **BLACK MOON**. The story starts... Once, many centuries ago, a black moon fell through the sky. Until it stopped. It stopped forever... here. At first, many people of the galaxy came to gaze at the black moon. For in those times it shone... a black light shone out of it. And the light of the black moon caught the people who gazed; and they could no longer think for themselves, or know right from wrong. At last the rulers of Space became worried about it. One day three of the mightiest and most powerful of them met together, and they decided that the black light of the moon would have to be put out. So they came to this place, to destroy the black moon. They covered up their faces. They tried... but they only made things worse! The black light of the moon escaped! And now even the mighty rulers were slaves to its power.

And that is how they are to this day (*indicating the platforms*). But (*getting up*)... it is also said that one day, through space there will come to the black moon a new energy, a new light... and this light will shine out through all the galaxies, and illuminate the whole Universe. And before that day arrives will come 'The Two'! (*she is back in front of the moon, standing between the prostrate NAUT and ASTRO).*

Yes, they have arrived at last. These are *(indicating R and L)* 'The Two'.

(The STORYTELLER sheds her air of high awe and mystery, and as ASTRO and NAUT come to consciousness she sits between them adopting a chatty style).

STORYTELLER: *(She waits for them to collect themselves)*: Take off your helmets!

ASTRO: *(He starts, trying to find the voice in the air)* No! We need them to breathe.

STORYTELLER: *(She is amused)* Why?

ASTRO: We can't breathe unless your atmosphere has enough oxygen.

STORYTELLER: Take off your helmets.

ASTRO: *(Furious with this elusive voice)* Don't be ridiculous! *(to NAUT)*...It's a trick.

NAUT: *(Who has seen the STORYTELLER from the beginning of consciousness)*... I believe her.

ASTRO: Who?

NAUT: Her.

ASTRO: You're a scientist. You can't believe anything, without evidence, and I can't see any here.

NAUT: Perhaps we are the evidence.

ASTRO: Us? You're crazy. Look, you haven't got concussion or anything have you?

NAUT: *(Interrupting)*... We've got to do something. We've lost contact with control... we've lost our way in space... and yet we're still alive. ·

ASTRO: Yes, and let's keep it that way.

NAUT: Astro, look at the evidence.

ASTRO: Don't be silly. The only thing I can see in front of me is this black thing... like a dead meteor ...

NAUT: Nothing else?

ASTRO: Oh, and her... (*double-take, as he realizes what he has said and seen*).

NAUT: We've got to communicate with her! (*to STORYTELLER*) Excuse me. You're probably wondering who we are. I'm Naut, and this is my colleague... Astro. We're space explorers, and our spacecraft, Zed II is... er... up there somewhere.

STORYTELLER: (*Charmed, offering a hand*): How do you do? (*she turns and offers her hand to ASTRO*).

ASTRO: (*Just about to take the hand offered*) Don't be stupid, Naut. There's no evidence that points to the existence of life in this galactic region. You probably knocked your head on a rock...

NAUT: (*A rare moment of impatience with ASTRO's stupidity*) I'm talking to the evidence, Astro.

ASTRO: (*Dumb-show, watched with amusement by STORYTELLER, as he attempts to touch the evidence... finally*): Ahhh! It's real.

STORYTELLER: (*Dryly*): Yes, I'm as real as you are.

ASTRO: What are you doing here?

STORYTELLER: Waiting for you; so that we can start the story again.

ASTRO: The story? What story? What do you mean, start the story again?

STORYTELLER: Well, it has to keep going. It never really ends, you know.

ASTRO: Bah! Bunkum! (*moves across C and takes NAUT DR*) I've never heard of a story that doesn't end, sometime or other. Really, what is going on, Naut, this is too much for a dedicated scientist like me (*moving back L*) I'm beginning to wish I'd stayed in ground operations... (*grumbles*).

NAUT: (*To STORYTELLER*): You mean... we're sort of in the middle of a story.

STORYTELLER: I knew you would understand. Sometimes it's different, and sometimes it's the same. You never

	really know... until it starts happening (*ASTRO is appalled*).
NAUT:	Er... has it been happening lately?
STORYTELLER:	(*Very serious*) Not for a while. That's why I was expecting you... 'The Two'.
ASTRO:	Evidence! Evidence! There's no sense to this, without evidence!
STORYTELLER:	(*Agreeably*): That's right. So the sooner we begin... the sooner you will have your evidence (*she produces a feather duster and disappears R, dusting the moon as though it were a piece of furniture*).
	(*ASTRO and NAUT move to each other*).
NAUT:	Oh, come on Astro. She looks like us. Despite those funny clothes. She speaks our language.
ASTRO:	It could have been monitored and decoded by a foreign intelligence.
STORYTELLER:	(*Appearing L, dusting*) But it was not! (*moves between NAUT and ASTRO with the duster as she speaks to NAUT*) Whatever language you speak, I speak it too. I am the same as you (*her storytelling style is reappearing*).
NAUT:	(*After a pause*) I trust you (*she takes off her helmet; places it next to the moon R*).
ASTRO:	(*Crosses to NAUT, business as he first examines her carefully... eye, pulse, etc.*) Evidence... I'm satisfied. (*removes helment, places it L*).
NAUT:	But where are we? You said that the story was waiting to happen.
STORYTELLER:	(*Urgently*) Oh, I am only the Storyteller, I have never been in the story when it happens... (*fade to quick BLACKOUT as the STORYTELLER disappears. During the blackout the actor must inhabit the LUNARIA costume DR. Lights fade up to dim only*).
ASTRO:	She's disappeared! Now what do we do?
NAUT:	(*Crossing to him*) What all our friends safe on earth at

	this moment would give their eye-teeth to be able to do! Examine a previously unexplored moon!
ASTRO:	Oh yes! I forgot. Well, come on then Naut... I'd better take charge *(he adopts an exploratory pose)* Follow me.
	(They commence stylized exploration C, R, and L. They are moving further L when, entering the field of PLANETORIA, both are suddenly frozen and simultaneously commence the humming noise indicated in the next speeches).
ASTRO:	Hmm... Stop that Hmm... ridiculous noise Naut Hmmmmmm.
NAUT:	Hmm... I can't stop it Astro... Hmm my throat seems to be stuck Hmmmmmm.
ASTRO:	Hmm Keep your mouth shut then Hennnnnnnnn.
NAUT:	Hmmmm What? Hmmmmm.
ASTRO:	*(Shouting)*: HMMMM KEEP YOUR MOUTH SHARHAaaaaaaaaa *(he can't shut it)*.
NAUT:	Ooohm, Astro youhm sound funny *(laughs)* Ha hmm Ha hrrrn Ha hmm Ha hrrrn... *(she has to keep laughing)*.
ASTRO:	*(Mighty physical effort)*: HAAAA this is HAAAA serious Naut HAAAAAAA *(he has managed to force his way. holding NAUT, out of the field. They burst away from the influence and collapse. As they pick themselves up and recover)*. What happened?
NAUT:	Something stopped us... like a force field. Only it tickled.
ASTRO:	*(Speaking his mind)* FORCE FIELDS DON'T TICKLE, NAUT! There's something that it's guarding... out there.
NAUT:	Or something in here.
ASTRO:	Eh?
NAUT:	Us.
ASTRO:	What!

NAUT: If there's a power circuit between these three... then we can't explore anywhere but right here. Have you thought of that?

ASTRO: Well, no, not yet, Naut. But no doubt I would have... if I'd had time to think about it... which I haven't (had yet etc.) ...

NAUT: Why don't we go in this direction, and find out?

ASTRO: *(Pause... then, emphatically)* You.

NAUT: What are you going to do?

ASTRO: My dear Naut. I shall make a scientific observation. Of what happens to you.

NAUT: *(Opens her mouth)*: HaHmm HaHmm HaHmm... oops! *(to ASTRO, amazed)* Did I make that noise?

ASTRO: You did.

NAUT: I couldn't help it.

ASTRO: Well, never mind about that. Just get over there and crash through!

NAUT: Wish me luck, Astro.

ASTRO: Go on, go on. Don't waste time *(he calls)* Take it by surprise!

(NAUT turns to nod her head at Astro before limbering up for her barrier-breaking run. She darts forward. Frozen as before. However, this time, LUNARIA comes alive; inclines towards Naut, making robot like gestures which NAUT has to mirror.)

NAUT: Help, Astro... Astro, help! I'm stuck!

ASTRO: *(Very pleased)* Good work, Naut! That should have closed the circuit. Now you stay there while I crash through over here *(limbering up... very macho)* This'll give 'em something to think about...

(He runs L and with a karate movement attempts to force himself through the barrier feet-first. However he is stopped as by an invisible wall. He collapses in a heap, humming as before.)

(A confusion of anxiety from both NAUT... gesturing... and ASTRO... humming. THE PRESIDENT OF SPACE comes alive UC, although it is merely turned slowly round to face the front by THE WARRIOR as he appears from behind it, stretching and yawning.)

WARRIOR: *(Coming forward, very sleepy at first but becoming brisk and business like)* Ahhhhh! Visitors, eh? *(to PRESIDENT, turning it back).* All right, all right. Leave them to me.

(He times his speech as he releases first NAUT and then ASTRO, hauling them back to their helmets where he drops them both on the ground in the collapsed state we have come to expect from time to time).

Come along. I'll have to make a bit of an enquiry into this. What's going on, eh? *(he has dumped NAUT... now listens to ASTRO)* Two of em, eh? Wonder what you've been up to? We'll soon see. Too bad for you - if you've been interfering *(he is now C between them; to both)* Come on, come on. You'd better sit up and tell me all about it.

NAUT: Ohhhhh.

(But ASTRO is furious)

ASTRO: Now look here, Mr HaaaaHaaaaHaaaaHaaaammm

WARRIOR: *(In a somewhat menacing tone)* Snap out of it *(shaking ASTRO)* Something's happened. Or I wouldn't have been woken up. You'd better tell me what it is.

NAUT: Where did you come from?

WARRIOR: Oh! I've been here all the time.

ASTRO: Not another one of them. Don't tell me. You're waiting for it all to start happening again. Because it hasn't really stopped. It's just waiting in the middle. Only there isn't any middle because it can't starthar har har harpening harp harp harp I mean happening haaaaaaaaaaaaaaa...

WARRIOR: *(Shaking him as before)* Relax!

NAUT: It'll be all right ASTRO. Take it easy.

ASTRO: Ohhhhh... I can't stand it.

NAUT: Why not? It's evidence.

ASTRO: (*Crosses in front of WARRIOR... lays hands around NAUT's neck perhaps*) I'll evidence you in a minute NAUT... Nahaha... Nahaha... Nahaha...

WARRIOR: (*Shaking ASTRO*) He'll get over it in a minute. It never lasts long after they release you.

NAUT: But you released us... didn't you?

WARRIOR: Oh no. I only brought you in here. They never move off there. That's why they woke me up.

NAUT: (*Thinking*): So you only wake up when something happens in the story.

ASTRO: (*Quietly*): Nahmha hmhaaaaaaa ....

WARRIOR: (*Shaking ASTRO as a matter of course*) That's right! Other times I have a good long sleep up there. I don't mind the ground; I've been a soldier all my life, and you can get used to anything when you have to. Mind you, I'd like to settle down some day... stay in the one spot for awhile, get to know the people; it was like that once

NAUT: When?

WARRIOR: When? Oh, once upon a time. I haven't always been on guard duty, you know, Back in another time I used to know those three quite well. We... er worked together you might say. In fact you could say that I was once a friend of theirs.

ASTRO: Let's get this straight Mr Her Hmm Har. You're a friend of them? Hem Hem Hem?

WARRIOR: (*Shaking him*) Once upon a time, we were all friends together.

ASTRO: (*In a panic*) Where's my helmet? (*dives for it; collapses over it; BLACKOUT, during which the actor inhabits the costume of THE PRESIDENT OF SPACE*).

NAUT: ASTRO! ASTRO! (*lights dim up*) Oh! (*anxiously*) He's disappeared!

WARRIOR: I wouldn't worry about him. He is probably upset because he can't understand the story.

NAUT: (*Frightened*) I wish I could!

WARRIOR: (*Expanding*) It's simple, really. This is how it was. Everything was all right, you see, until this (*gesture to moon*) turned up. Or rather, it would have been all right... if they hadn't turned nasty... (*he is not getting very far with it*).

NAUT: It sounded different when the Storyteller told us.

WARRIOR: What did she tell you?

NAUT: About the Black Moon! About how it stopped here. Forever. And about a black light that used to shine out of it...

WARRIOR: Oh, that's only her version of the story. What she doesn't know she makes up.

NAUT: Really?

WARRIOR: For a start, what she doesn't know is that this thing is always on the move. It's never in one place for as long as forever. Well, nothing really stays still out here in space... although it might seem like it. And wherever that goes... they go. And wherever they go... I go.

NAUT: That's right! People at home used to think our planet stopped still in space, while the sun and the moon went round it.

WARRIOR: Now let me guess. You'd be from Earth, wouldn't you, with a story like that! What century is it there now... the twenty first?

(*NAUT nods*) We haven't been near Earth for... oh, a thousand years or so. The last time we were there, people called it the Dark Ages (*laughs*) We left in a hurry that time... they blamed us for the Black Death, though we really had nothing to do with that. As you Earth people found out later, that was caused by rats, and by people not cleaning up their rubbish properly. People will always try to

	find someone else to blame for the mess they make themselves.
NAUT:	I suppose they do! But do you think the Storyteller's story wasn't true?
WARRIOR:	I won't say it's true or it's not true. It's another kind of story
NAUT:	And your story is different?
WARRIOR:	More like what actually happened. My story's got more facts in it.
NAUT:	I wish ASTRO were here to listen to that.
WARRIOR:	Oh he's listening all right. No-one ever completely disappears, out here.
NAUT:	So the Storyteller's here too?
WARRIOR:	Yes, but that's the difference. She doesn't listen.
NAUT:	I wish I could remember how her story started. 'One day three of the mightiest and most powerful rulers met in Space ... '
WARRIOR:	(*Interrupting*) Three, she told you? That's something else she's made up. It wasn't like that at all. There weren't three of them, there were four.
NAUT:	How can you be so sure there were four?
WARRIOR:	Because I was there. Because I saw it happen. And because... I was the fourth.
NAUT:	But it all happened centuries ago. The Storyteller said so. At least I remember that much.
WARRIOR:	So you believe her... without hearing my story?
NAUT:	Well... ?
WARRIOR:	You are an astronaut. You believe that you can't live in space without your space-helmet. And yet, a little while ago, you took it off... because the Storyteller said so.
NAUT:	You're right (*runs D, and to and fro*) This is a dead moon... a burnt out piece of space matter. There

can't be any atmosphere here (*panics, as ASTRO did*) I need... my helmet! (*runs for it, collapses*).

(*BLACKOUT... during which the actress inhabits the PLANETORIA costume. Light cues come up for the re-enactment*).

WARRIOR: Now, instead of being in the story yourself, you must watch. This is how it was.

(*SOUND and LIGHT effects*).

(*During this sequence, movement is in a formalized circular sweep around the Moon. It may be arrested or speeded up according to the needs of the dialogue*).

LUNARIA: From Lunaria I come (*moves upstage*).
PLANETORIA: From Planetoria, I (*to WARRIOR*) And you?
WARRIOR: From Arthura the Brilliant, whose beams
Flood full the empty caverns of the sky with light.
PRESIDENT: My fellow kings and presidents of Space,
I welcome you to this our Summit meeting.
There is an urgent problem we must face;
Therefore I will dispense with courteous greeting.
For some time now, too many of our people
Have disappeared; the cause lies in this place.
LUNARIA: Lunaria a has suffered this most badly.
Parties of tourists, out on holiday
To visit families on neighbour moons, tell sadly
Of friends who travelled here to view this moon
And haven't yet returned.
PLANETORIA: Oh, its's the same on Planetoria.
If anything, more serious.
A spaceship full of our geologists,
Coming to study the surface of this moon
Has not been seen again.
PRESIDENT: What says the Warrior King of Arthura?
Do your enlightened citizens yet know
Of any reason to mistrust this moon?
WARRIOR: It's true, good President, I cannot here

	Report of any mishaps we have had.
	I think that none of us have idled by
	To stare upon this dull, black burnt out moon.
PLANETORIA:	Our best geologists! They've disappeared,
	They're scientists... not idle pleasure seekers.
LUNARIA:	Lunarians who came on holidays
	Were trying to enjoy their well-earned rest.
	For we Lunarians are known to be
	The hardest workers in our galaxy.
PLANETORIA:	As people who'll do anything for kicks
	Lunarians all are known as... Lunatics.
PRESIDENT:	My friends and fellow rulers, quarrel not.
	This is a matter where we should unite...
	Not play at hitting one another out.
	Come! Raise your hands. We'll summon here
	The latent power of electricity!

(The others now all congregate around the PRESIDENT's platform, where they all form a moving group suggestive of an electo-turbine.)

PLANETORIA:	Now, to destroy the power of this black moon
	I join my will with you all equally.
LUNARIA:	So the black moon will perish without trace
	I share my power in solidarity.
WARRIOR:	To banish the darkness from our galaxy,
	I lend the light of Arthura the Brilliant.

(The characters form a tableau UC.)

PRESIDENT:	Now with all power together in one place
	We strike as one, with arms resilient.

(Slow and stylized electrical ZOTS from the characters towards the moon.)

PRESIDENT:	Again! We'll stem this moon's black, evil tide!

(Another fusillade of electrical ZOTS. Blinking lights brilliant with colour from inside the Moon. The CROWN rises.)

WARRIOR: The evil light's escaping from inside!

(After this point, all but the WARRIOR; succumb at various times to the moon's powers.)

LUNARIA: Treasure I see! To keep Lunaria
Richly endowed forever Queen of Space.

PLANETORIA: KNOWLEDGE! Enough for Planetoria
Possessing it, to outwit everyone.

PRESIDENT: Such Power shines here! Our unity is gone...
I feel danger... Yet I see the power!

WARRIOR: See it for what it is! The darkening power! The power of ignomy, pride, dishonour, greed.

LUNARIA: This light is rich, and I must have it all.

PLANETORIA: This light is knowledge, it must all be mine.

PRESIDENT: This light is power. Now power must be my creed.

(Knocking aside the WARRIOR from their ranks, the other three commence an intense circling of the Moon, from which no attempt by the WARRIOR can deflect them.)

WARRIOR: I beg you all, consider what you do!
If what you say is true, then all of us
Should share this burden and this happiness;
So that our people progress equally,
Not one at the expense of others.
Come, let's sit down then, here, before the moon,
And like the friends and allies that we are,
Consider slowly what is best to do!

LUNARIA: I cannot wait.

PLANETORIA: I dare not miss this chance.

PRESIDENT: I will act now!

(While the WARRIOR crouches and hides his eyes downstage, the others remove tokens from the Crown, which they display. As this is done, THE IMPRISONED QUEEN rises inside the Moon. While the others kneel by the Moon, the QUEEN, her arm movements suggesting turmoil, sings.)

Frank Sutherland Davidson

(N.B. In a cast of four, the Queen's voice must be taped, unless STORYTELLER/LUNARIA can mange the U.C.)

THE QUEEN: *(Sings)* I am the imprisoned Queen
Sorrow and confusion
Mark where I have been.

From this black and ugly Moon
Confusion spreads about
And sorrow follows soon.

The power of darkness has confined me here;
Yet nothing can destroy the Crown I wear;

Because these Three have taken
An old power from my Crown
The light shall re-awaken.

A new life to replace me;
This Moon shall disappear:
Everyone shall know

The joy and harmony of peace and love,
All people dance and sing, below, above.

(The QUEEN sinks out of sight into the Moon. The Three move haltingly and trance-like, to their respective platforms, where the actors must be ready on the blackout to dehabit, and to re-assume the roles of ASTRO, NAUT and STORYTELLER. Only the WARRIOR is left.)

WARRIOR: What have you done? My friends are all beguiled,
Release them, they are mighty rulers here,
The galaxy will suffer for their loss.

THE QUEEN: Their violence
Has made them prisoners bound.
You, Warrior, stand sentry on this ground
Until they learn this truth: that violence makes
More pain for he who gives it, than who takes.

WARRIOR: But how are they to learn?
And I'm to be sentry...
It'll be... forever...

(BLACKOUT. Exit WARRIOR. When the Moon spots come up again, enter ASTRO and NAUT from behind the

Moon. Their helmets have remained on stage through the preceding scene.)

NAUT: Did you see that?

ASTRO: Did you hear it?

NAUT: We heard the story.

ASTRO: And we saw the story.

NAUT: Now do you believe?

ASTRO: I don't know! What was the name of that chap we were talking to?

NAUT: 'WARRIOR King of Arthura the Brilliant'. Have you heard of it?

ASTRO: It wasn't in my space atlas when I was at school.

NAUT: Neither were... what were their names... Lunaria and Planetoria.

ASTRO: And what about him! *(pointing upstage to PRESIDENT).*

NAUT: He took some of the Crown too.

ASTRO: *(Suffering from complexity of feeling)* Maybe he's still got it.

NAUT: Of course. Everyone has. That's what's wrong.

ASTRO: Well, they ought to put it back then.

NAUT: *(Turning to the Moon)* Yes! That's probably what the voice meant.

ASTRO: Look out! Don't interfere with it!

(But NAUT has tapped the surface of the Moon... like a geologist perhaps... and from inside it there commences a loud ticking sound, not unlike the sound of a geiger counter or a bomb. If possible the Moon might rock slightly to and fro now.)

(ASTRO panics and runs around the perimeter, collecting the hum from PLANETORIA... through which he burbles... and the robot movements from LUNARIA. As he passes the

PRESIDENT upstage, this figure is activated as before; as the WARRIOR enters from behind. NAUT has disappeared.)

(ASTRO is coming DL but is being overtaken by slow motion, so that the WARRIOR overtakes him and deals with him as before during the following).

WARRIOR: *(Very sleepy at first)* Ahhhhhh! *(yawns)* Visitors, eh? All right, all right. Leave them to me. Come along. I'll have to make a bit of an enquiry into this *(he is depositing ASTRO near the latter's helmet, L)* What's going on, eh? *(he yawns and retires, re-setting the PRESIDENT as he goes).*

STORYTELLER: And so 'The Two' have come to the Black Moon. Yes, this is how it was *(she inspects ASTRO, who when she touches him regains consciousness)* and so the story starts ... *(she goes to touch NAUT R, but of course cannot find her. The STORYTELLER is put off her stroke and the ensuing scene is frenetic and surreal, like a speeded-up movie.)* Once... many centurie's ago...

ASTRO: It's all wrong!

STORYTELLER: A Black Moon fell through the sky...

ASTRO: We're supposed to go forward!

STORYTELLER: Until it stopped, it stopped forever here ...

ASTRO: No, no, that's all over...

STORYTELLER: *(Very quickly indeed)*: At first many people of the galaxy came to gaze at it for in those times it shone, a black light shone out of it ...

ASTRO: *(Speaking over her to audience)* I've got to stop her! We'll never put things right if she just goes on telling the wrong story over and over again! We're not getting anywhere!

STORYTELLER: And the light of the Black Moon caught the people who gazed and they could no longer think for themselves or know right from wrong ... at last the rulers of Space became worried One day three of the mightiest and most powerful of them met together.

ASTRO: THAT'S WHERE YOU'RE WRONG! I'll tell the story...

(As ASTRO takes the stage, the STORYTELLER, fading and slowing down, whirls away behind the Moon...)

ASTRO: One day the President of Space called a Summit meeting. Here... Lunaria came to it. She was a bit of a dill but a hard worker and she got annoyed when Planetoria... that one... called her a Lunatic *(ASTRO gets a slight attack of the hums)* HmHa HmHa HmHa... I suppose it's funny when you come to think of it *(he clears his throat and continues)* Planetoria herself was as stuck up as they come... she thought she had all the right answers... you know the type. Oh, and 'WARRIOR King of Arthura' came too. He's up there somewhere. Nobody ever really disappears out here in Space... *(an attack of the robot Lunarian movements is imminent. ASTRO's cool is in danger. He runs around the area... in the opposite direction from last time... calling for NAUT on a rising, wild inflection).*

ASTRO: NAUT! NAUT!

(NAUT appears from behind the Moon, joining on to ASTRO's progression around it so that it should remind the audience of their first entry).

NAUT: *(As they circle and turn)* Are you all right ASTRO?

ASTRO: You get used to it, you know!

NAUT: *(As they slow down and find their places, L and R)*. Astro, I think I've made a very important discovery.

ASTRO: *(Generously)*: Well, we both have, Naut. The Intergalactic Space Council will be very interested in this, and I'll see to it that your name is mentioned.

NAUT: NO! Something even more important....

ASTRO: Eh?

NAUT: We can see what really happened in the story of this moon, so many centuries ago...

ASTRO: My dear Naut. That's not new to me. Why, I distinctly remember, a moment ago, trying to tell that Storyteller...

NAUT: That's it! She can't!

ASTRO: Ha ha, you don't have to tell me... hopeless at it, she was...

NAUT: ASTRO! WE'RE IN THE STORY.

ASTRO: What?

NAUT: Whatever we do... makes the story happen.

ASTRO: Oh, really, NAUT...

NAUT: We must be... 'The Two'!

ASTRO: The who?

NAUT: 'Before the new "light comes will come The Two! (*she is quoting*).

ASTRO: You mean... that's us?

NAUT: Let's prove it, ASTRO. Now.

ASTRO: My dear NAUT, Haste. Haste is the enemy of all proper scientific enquiry ... (*is he actually frightened?*)

NAUT: Rubbish, ASTRO, I can't wait to see whether I'm right.

ASTRO: (*Pretending to leave*). No, I can't either

NAUT: (*Collaring him*). The important thing is to understand how it all works.

ASTRO: Yeee-es.

NAUT: Now. The WARRIOR's their sentry. He got that job at the time of the calamity. Right?

ASTRO: Right.

NAUT: But he doesn't go on duty until he gets a signal. Right?

ASTRO: Right.

NAUT: From that one... the President. That's the one we have to defuse.

ASTRO: Defuse? That one? Why?

NAUT:	ASTRO, he was the President of Space. But he's been caught like the others and he's never going to be any different unless we do something to reverse the power.
ASTRO:	I suppose you're right. Like the storyteller can't help but tell the same story.
NAUT:	That's it! You and I are going to finish the story.
ASTRO:	How?
NAUT:	Now, ASTRO, we need facts. How do you break an electric circuit?
ASTRO:	*(Back in his element)* Simple, NAUT.. Find the battery, and disconnect it.
NAUT:	Then that's our mission.
ASTRO:	Well, what are we waiting for? Let's see. The messages have to go from both of these before he reacts. So what would happen if we take him by surprise.
NAUT:	One of us must get close enough to examine him.
ASTRO:	Right. And it should be me.
NAUT:	Not me?
ASTRO:	No. We're working on your theory, and you should be in charge.
NAUT:	Thanks, ASTRO.
ASTRO:	Well... Good luck, NAUT.
NAUT:	*(Copying his manner)*: Go on, go on. Don't waste time.
	(ASTRO commences to sneak up on the PRESIDENT. Some play can be made out of feints and starts. Eventually though the figure begins to turn as before. ASTRO is immobilized UC. Enter the WARRIOR as before).
WARRIOR:	Ahhhh! All right, all right. leave them to me *(he touches the immobilized ASTRO as before he had touched the PRESIDENT; registers some abnormality though he is not yet into the context).*

WARRIOR:	What's going on?
NAUT:	We're trying to help you.
WARRIOR:	I'll have to make a bit of an enquiry
NAUT:	(*In a loud voice commanding and heroic style*): Warrior! King of the Brilliant Planet! (*aside*) Oh, I hope that's right.
WARRIOR:	(*A subtle change of character*) What did you say?
NAUT:	(*Aside*). I think it's going to work! WARRIOR, the time has come To end your vigil here. Through Space we've come, ASTRO and NAUT, Two scientists of Earth: Help us and trust us; join with us To solve the Black Moon's mystery.
WARRIOR:	(*As above*) Your words are like an echo of an old story. I feel I know you well ...
NAUT:	There's something new to happen. We're going on... we're travelling forward. Together we'll find the ending of this plight.
WARRIOR:	Who are you? Not The One who brings the light?
NAUT:	No. ASTRO and I together are 'The Two'.
WARRIOR:	The Two! I remember! You came wearing helmets. You doubted. And you demanded evidence (*he fetches the immobilized ASTRO to his helmet L.*) So you had to watch our story. (*ASTRO quickly comes to consciousness and gets up*).
NAUT:	We've got to move fast.
WARRIOR:	I am myself again! My deeds my own, No longer subject of the moon's black will. The power can be broken... the energy reversed. Let's put our thoughts together, and our arms. (*Led by the WARRIOR, they form another version of the electo-turbine*). Together now, we go to conquer darkness,

	Our wills joined equally, our powers shared.
NAUT:	ASTRO and NAUT, two scientists of Earth Join with the WARRIOR King of Arthura.
ASTRO:	To bring the power of light back to this place.
ALL:	Release your prisoners! Let us see your face.
	(From the top of the Moon, the CROWN is seen again as the QUEEN rises. This time she is played by the STORYTELLER and must be seen).
THE QUEEN:	*(Sings).* Goodbye to dark, It is the other side of light. In every spark
	There is a glimmer of the might That lives beyond all galaxies
	Swelling the farthest caverns of the sky; More timeless than the moons and seas
	Gentle as birds asleep in trees Sleep in the dark before the the morning:
	Welcome the light; new day is dawning, Goodbye to dark.
	(The QUEEN removes her mask or veil, to reveal herself as the STORYTELLER).
NAUT:	It is... the Storyteller!
THE QUEEN:	Not yet. I am what is to be, But still also what has been.
	(She replaces her mask or veil).
	Now my work is done This crown is handed on. Astronauts of Earth Convey it to the place Where the One who will replace me Comes through Space.
	(The QUEEN takes off her crown and raises it above her head. ASTRO and NAUT on either side, take it. The QUEEN sinks and exits from the Moon unseen. ASTRO

	and NAUT bring the Crown down towards the audience).
ASTRO:	My word, NAUT, it's brilliant. Why, look in here. You can see all the facts that go together to make up all the galaxies... the secret of the Universe...
NAUT:	One fact at a time, ASTRO. This belongs to the new ruler of Space.
ASTRO:	But if I were to take out...- just one of these crystals... and look at it... through a microscope of course...
NAUT:	*(In final authority)* No, ASTRO.
	(The MOON is leaving. As it rises, and the Moon spots fade, spot on the PRESIDENT's platform UC comes up to reveal WARRIOR and STORYTELLER seated or standing there habited as the new rulers of Space. They come downstage in processional. One of them receives the Crown. The majestic sounds of a space coronation. EXIT OMNES.)

Frank Sutherland Davidson

LONGER ONE-ACT PLAYS

Like its literary cousin the short story, the one-act play functions differently from its big brother/sister the full-length play.

Generally, the one-acter centres on one specific problem, crisis or turn of plot. The climax deals with the adjustment of this central situation. The consequence of the adjustment is presented in the play's conclusion.

The first of the following plays, "Telling Barbie", centres on a social situation involving emotional honesty; "Bush Dreaming", the second, focusses on spiritual awareness and responsibility.

Frank Sutherland Davidson

TELLING BARBIE

A social comedy set in 1980's Sydney.

Cast: LARRY, *an aggressive businessman,*
JACK, a used car dealer, late fifties or early sixties,
DAPH, Jack's wife, broad Australian accent,
JANE, Sydney socialite, pretentious and overbearing,
DOUG, Jane's husband, 'old money',
JANEICE, an attractive professional woman, over thirty.

Setting: *The late 1980's - early 1990's in Larry's flat in Surry Hills, Sydney. Centre - a curtained wall with a well-stocked bar in front of it. Door to bedroom and bathroom (L) Front door side (R). Dried flower arrangements everywhere. LARRY (C) is farewelling JACK and DAPH.*

LARRY: Well... it's been... interesting... seeing you again... Jack... Daph... *(he shakes hands with them, trying to negotiate with them to the front door).*

JACK: *(Not offering to go)* Gees, Larry, I said to Daph, 'Larry must've gone off his rocker. How could he walk out and leave a beautiful little girl like Barbie, there's gotta be something at the bottom, you mark my words.'

DAPH: Yes, we were that sorry that you and Barbie have got personal troubles between the two of you, Larry, I said to Jack...

JACK: You can count on us, mate.

DAPH: Living next door, we've got that fond of you both, I said to Jack, 'Jack, if any other woman's come between Larry and that dear little Barbie, I'll take to her with my bare fists, I will too,' I said, didn't I Jack.

LARRY: Thanks, Daph...

DAPH: And it isn't even as if you two had any kiddies, is it Larry?

LARRY: Er... no. Look, thanks for coming round...

DAPH: Yes, and you come round to our place, Larry. Real soon. You'll get a glimpse of Barbie doing the washing up in her kitchen through our venetians...

LARRY: Oh. Good to know you've got close neighbours. Look. Thanks for dropping in...

JACK: That's OK mate... (*shakes hands again*). When things straighten out, we'll all get together... (*Laughs a cheering-up laugh*).

LARRY: (*Laughs too*) Sure! Just like when we first moved to Randwick. Daph... (*kisses her... which DAPH obviously enjoys*).

DAPH: Oooh!

JACK: (*Not entirely pleased*) Come on love.

DAPH: Goodbye Larry. Look after yourself dear.

LARRY: So long... (*shuts door*) Phew!

(*LARRY leans against the door. Then moves C to bar, lights a cigarette and pours himself a large drink. Picks up telephone and dials*).

LARRY: (*Eagerly*) Janeice?? (*then flat*) Oh. Bugger. Janeice... just ring me, please, as soon as you get this. Can't wait to hear from you. (*He hangs up and stubs out cigarette. The doorbell rings.*) Oh jeezus. (*He goes to open it*).

(*ENTER DOUG and JANE*).

JANE: Darling! (*kisses him, moving C*) I must say, it's very courageous of you, to leave little Barbie at the mercy of those terrible country boys in town for the polo, I hope you're not thinking of leaving me darling, actually I can't think of anything more delicious now I come to think of it... (*and sits*).

DOUG: (*Shakes hands*) We can't stay long, Larry. We're on our way to dinner and then a show at the Opera House, why don't you come along with us?

LARRY: Thanks Doug but at the moment I'm so pissed off I couldn't sit through anything less than one of those transcendental meditation sessions.

JANE:	What a terribly good idea, darling, they have the most awful incense, that's to cure people of smoking, so *(waving to clear the air)* it'd be ideal for you. I must mention it to Barbie, when I see her at lunch tomorrow.
LARRY:	*(Surprised)* Are you having lunch with Barbie tomorrow?
JANE:	Well, naturally, darling, you can't expect the girl not to call on her friends in a time of crisis, *(to DOUG)* so darling you'll just have to take your mother to the Opera on your own tomorrow night.
DOUG:	What!
JANE:	Us girls are going to Janeice's place at Vaucluse for a get-together.
DOUG:	Do you really think I'm going to take Mother to the Opera?
JANE:	Of course darling.
DOUG:	On my own?
JANE:	Absolutely.
DOUG:	Not on your life... I'd rather die.
JANE:	Oh darling. How utterly courageous.
DOUG:	Look. If you women are having one of your pow-wows, I'm having a night out. How about it, Larry, meet me at seven and we can have a drink before dinner.
LARRY:	I haven't settled in here yet, and I just want to have an early night tomorrow.
JANE:	*(Rises)* Darling, you look as though you've been here a year, *(she waves at the dried arrangements)* the place has been through the most frightful drought, doesn't it make you feel excruciatingly thirsty, you must be dried to a cinder... *(she moves meaningfully towards the bar)*.
LARRY:	What'll it be? For a quick one? Doug?

JANE: He'll have a Scotch. I'll have a double brandy. I must say, Larry, I was surprised when I heard that Barbie had asked you to leave.

DOUG: (*Heartily*) Oh, Jane's always telling me to get lorst, but there'd be a terrible stink if I actually went orf with someone else...

JANE: (*Taking her drink and moving downstage*) Darling, I don't remember a terrible stink that time when you and Mary Fisher were marooned in the Florida Hotel at Terrigal and you just happened to find Mary cooling her heels while her husband was in Fiji... God knows what he was cooling at the time, he'd freeze a raging bushfire to death... cheers everybody... (*she drinks*).

DOUG: I've told you, Jane, I caught three bream and seven tailor that weekend. You ate most of them yourself. And you know Mary doesn't like fishing.

JANE: (*Gives him a slow and meaningful look*) No. But she is very experienced in baiting her hook.

LARRY: (*Doorbell rings... he looks at watch*)... oh god... no... (*cautiously opens door, revealing JACK and DAPH*) Er...

JACK: Well, Larry old son! I said to Daph, 'Gees, I feel crook, goin' off and leavin' the old Larry on his own, we shoulda stayed to cheer him up...

DAPH: Besides, Jack and I were just off to the trots, and I said to Jack, 'Maybe Larry'd like to have a flutter on the horses,' so we came back to get you (*confidentially*) Jack's got a real hot tip for the fifth race...

JACK: I brought along a few tubes, where's your fridge, Larry, I'll put 'em in, maybe we can crack one or two before we leave.

LARRY: Well, it's certainly a surprise to see you again but...

JACK: That's OK Larry me boy, (*gives him the beer carton while he extracts tins*) you just hang onto this while I open 'em up and we'll get stuck into a bit of cheer. What about yous two?

LARRY: Oh, ar, Doug, Jane, these are my... er... neighbours Jack and Daphne Walker... Jack and Daph, meet the Fitzgibbons.

DOUG: (*Shakes hands with JACK*) How do you do old chap... glad to meet another punter. Have a go on the gee gees meself from time to time... (*Bows to DAPH*) Mrs Walker.

DAPH: Oh how nice to meet you Mr Fitzgibbon, and Mrs Fitzgibbon too of course... my word, in that frock of yours, you look just like my Kylie, only older of course, she's twenty-one next month and she's that excited, we're giving her a big party for all her friends, all her friends from the Art and Fashion School that is, and just a few of our old cronies to keep me and Jack company... I know! Why don't you all come along to the party too! We'd love to have you...

JACK: That's right, help us get rid of the beer. These young fry seem to go for nothing but all this fancy stuff, Bacardi and the like. Pickles your guts and puts a hole in your poopoo valve... (*nudges JANE*).

DAPH: Ooh, Jack, you are awful...

JACK: (*To JANE*) Come on love, you might as well have a drop of the liquid amber, put a flush in your boo-doir...

JANE: Thank you Mr Walker, I believe I'll have another double brandy. No soda.

LARRY: Here, let me... (*he goes to the bar*) The Walkers are two of my oldest friends...

JANE: We were just reminiscing with Larry about old times, Mr Walker...

JACK: Call me Jack, love!

JANE: ... and we were apparently coming to the conclusion that old friendships irrigate the soul. What do you think?

JACK: Which one, love... the hay-soul, or the har-soul? (*laughs immoderately*)

DAPH: Ooh, Jack, you are awful. I know! Why don't we all make a night of it? The five of us! After the trots, Jack and me often go to a lovely little Chinese café in Dixon Street for a chow min... and then up the Cross for one of those terrible strip shows, Jack insists, but he seems to enjoy it, and I must say, it can be a real giggle, some of the things they get up to...

DOUG: And get down to, Mrs Walker, eh?

DAPH: (*Overcome with giggles*) Oooooh, Mr FitzGibbons, you are aw...

JANE: I must say, Douglas, I'm glad you don't take me to any of these terrible strip shows. It would be too much to see them getting down to it.

DOUG: Darling, anything that proved too much for you I have yet to see.

JACK: (*Finishing his beer*) That's the spirit mate. Keep the womenfolk amused. Well, Larry... the trots'll be over if we don't get under way... are you a candidate?

LARRY: I'm staying put tonight. I'd like some time to settle in.

DAPH: So nice to have met you Mrs FitzGibbon... we'll see more of you, I know, at our Kylie's party! And Mr Fitzgibbon... any time you're over our way, next door to where Larry and Barbie live, you'll know our house, the one with the aboriginal bird bath and matching letterbox...

JACK: (*Pulling her towards the door*) Come on love.

DAPH: Goodbye Larry. Look after yourself dear... (*embraces and kisses LARRY*).

JACK: (*Displeased, warningly*) Daph! (*he pulls her away and they exit*).

LARRY: So long... (*shuts door*).

JANE: My dear! With friends like that, who needs TV.

LARRY: Old Jack's a bit rough round the edges... got the clues though. He's making a fortune out of used

	cars. Can be very entertaining when he's got a few in.
JANE:	He reminds me so terribly of poor Rosemary's first husband... you know, the one who spits when he speaks.
DOUG:	I say, Jane, he doesn't really you know. After all, he is an old Kings boy.
JANE:	(*To LARRY*) Didn't he offer to meet you at dawn with pistols drawn? You know... that time when you were found in Rosemary's flat with no clothes on. Frightfully early in the morning, as I recall.
LARRY:	Sounds like a figment of your over-fertile imagination Jane.
JANE:	(*Amused*) Really, darling... don't pretend that your little affair with Rosemary never happened. Barbie told me all about it... only a year after you two were married, too.
LARRY:	(*Annoyed*) Well, what if it did, it wasn't serious, and it only happened because Barbie insisted on working all hours on those ridiculous market research jobs... Look... this is really none of your business, Jane, I've never talked about it to anyone...
JANE:	Oh darling, unfortunately there's always a first time for everything.
LARRY:	I thought that if I went into business on my own, that she'd have... scope. You know... business contacts... lots of entertaining... well, it didn't work out like that. All that happened was that we starved for three months until the clients started coming in, and then, out of the blue, she went off and got herself a job. Said she was bored. Trouble was, she got so good at that damned job that (*sarcastic*) they couldn't do without her...
JANE:	So, darling? How does this little story end up with Rosemary?
LARRY:	Well, I just noticed Rosemary sort of hanging around, and so, I suppose you could say, I had a fling (*gyrating his hips*).

JANE: (*Screams*) A fling! Darling, you practically performed a full-length ballet, from what I can make out.

DOUG: Know how you feel, old sport. During the mining boom I didn't go near the boat for nearly three weeks. But look here... we really ought to be pushing orf... sure you don't want to come with us?

LARRY: I've still got a few things to unpack...

(*Phone rings*)

LARRY: Oh. Er... Hello? Barbie! Yes, this is the number I gave you. The flat? It's very comfortable. Of course it's got a bed. Well I haven't actually done a lot of, er, sleeping in it yet. Visitors? Of course. Do you expect me to go into a monastery? (*shouts*) I said a monastery! Why don't you shut up for long enough for me to tell you something (*shouts*) I didn't say sell you something, I said... Look, I didn't mean... (*looks at phone*).

JANE: Oh, you pig, it serves you right. No wonder she asked you to leave her. You certainly haven't changed. Will I ever forget what you put me through... (*waving her empty glass at LARRY*) another brandy, thank you... thank god I woke up in time and married Doug instead, what a deliverance.

DOUG: What?! Do you mean to say... you can't mean... I mean you don't mean to say... that you... you two turned on together? Well, well! You never told me this, Jane.

JANE: It was before I met you, darling, and principally because it made so little impression on me darling that I'd completely forgotten it... until this moment.

DOUG: Well, I'll be damned (*to LARRY*) Well, old boy. The two of you must have a lot to talk about... I'm going out for some peanuts. Won't be long. Bye bye!

LARRY: Don't be an ass, Doug. I've got some potato crisps here... (*gives DOUG an armful*).

JANE: Besides, darling, Larry was never great shakes as a lover. Too passionate. I prefer the bucolic type. They can be so desperately romantic.

LARRY:	(*Laughing*) Will you ever forget when I took you to Pokolbin for a tour of the wineries... that drunk Italian who poured a glass of pinot noir down your cleavage...
JANE:	Oh, wasn't he sweet, darling. And that winter, in Thredbo... when that divine Austrian ski instructor serenaded me under my window.
LARRY:	Our window!
JANE:	... and then tried to climb the balcony!
LARRY:	Yeah, he got a shock when I pushed him off and sent him rolling down the hill, into the car park... (*they laugh*).
JANE:	(*She finishes laughing*) H'm. He was drunk, of course, the beast (*indicates to remind Larry of her empty glass*).
LARRY:	Sorry... (*he refills her glass and his own*).
DOUG:	Well. Old home week, I see.
JANE:	Oh, we never set up house, darling. Purely a long-gone holiday affair.
LARRY:	Or an affair for holidays!
JANE:	Your so-called sense of humour! That was the real killer.
LARRY:	You could never see the funny side of all that beauty treatment you used to give yourself... seven kinds of skincream and a separate lotion for each wrinkle.
JANE:	You are a beast, Larry, and that was no reason to refer to me as a pickled passionfruit. I happen to have very good skin.
DOUG:	Look here, Larry, Jane has got very good skin.
LARRY:	Of course she has, mate.
DOUG:	Ahem. I think if you don't mind I'll have another drink after all... (*DOUG goes behind the bar and helps himself very generously*).
LARRY:	Right you are, Kitchener... (*he salutes*).
JANE:	Oh, you anarchist, Larry. That's really the trouble

LARRY:	with you, you know... you thrive on emotional disorder. And I suppose that's really why Barbie is fed up with you.

LARRY:	No. It isn't. I might as well tell you... but I want you to keep it quiet. I've had an offer for my business that I can't refuse. If it comes through we'll be set up for life. She can give up that stupid job of hers and have a flat in London, or New York, and she can do whatever she wants (*he moves*) And do you know what she said to me? That she didn't want any of it! That all she wanted was to settle down to family life. Settle down! Family life! What's that, I ask you! With a fortune at her fingertips, she wants to settle down! Well, that's when I told her that if she wanted to settle down, I wanted to take off... and if she wasn't willing to come, then I'd have to take off without her.

JANE:	(*Mock serious*) And she didn't throw herself on the ground and kiss your foot? Oh, poor Larry.

DOUG:	Now why would Barbie want to kiss Larry's foot Jane. She's got a great deal more taste than that.

LARRY:	I tell you what, I'm going to have a ball. The ball of the century. And none of this art and culture routine! It'll be Ascot, Le Mans, Barcelona for the bullfights... oh I'll be the tourist supreme. And make another fortune in international real estate while I'm at it too. After all, if you've got money to burn, what can you do with it except make more of it? People expect that. And you keep the economy is shape. The way I look at it, there's got to be a bit of every type in the world or we don't have a world. Low brow and high liquidity, that's me. I may be a low flier... but I'm sure going to have a lot of happy landings!

DOUG:	Jolly interesting view of life, old boy. Wouldn't mind taking up flying again meself, actually... if I could get away from the Stock Exchange for long enough.

JANE:	Larry, I wouldn't put it past you to start printing your own banknotes. And before that happens I must eat something. The beastly Oyster Bar, I

	expect, darling, or we'll miss the show at the Opera House completely.
DOUG:	Right you are, dearest. Larry, ring me up tomorrow about three and we'll arrange dinner.
LARRY:	Well, tomorrow... (*Phone rings*) Excuse me. Hello? Oh! (*pause*) No, I can't at the moment. Yes, soon. Can you hang on? I'll be able to talk in a minute. Right... (*puts down receiver, does not hang up*).
JANE:	Darling, how mysterious!
DOUG:	Jane, do come on. If you don't hurry I'll leave you here.
JANE:	Larry, at least come and see us before you jet out. We'll give you a send off in Double Bay... let us know when you decide to leave... Bye!
DOUG:	Bye! (*they EXIT*).
	(*LARRY shuts the door, goes back to the phone and picks up receiver*).
LARRY:	Janeice? Where are you? Oh, in the car... you're just around the corner then. You'll be here very soon? Right. (*puts phone down. Doorbell rings*) What the... (*he opens door to reveal DOUG and JANE, they move to C*).
LARRY:	Oh no!
DOUG:	Shan't be a moment old chap. Jane forgot her wrap. Where did you put it m'dear?
JANE:	Perhaps it's in the car after all... and in any case, I must go to the loo... shan't be a tick... (*EXITS to bathroom*).
LARRY:	(*Yells after her*) Just hurry up, will you! (*begins moving around the room, tidying up*).
DOUG:	Bear up old fellow. You're very edgy. You know, you could do with something to make you sleep. Always take a hip flask, meself, if I'm camping out on the boat... never forget one time up on the Hawkesbury it was, had a few nips, the mullet were biting, Jane and I were hauling them in hand over fist... I was just about to start the motor and head for home,

Frank Sutherland Davidson

	tripped over the bloody anchor chain and went headfirst into the water. Jane nearly killed herself laughing. Struck me on the head with the boathook, I remember, trying to get me out. And then... guess what...
LARRY:	No idea. I suppose you took a nip out of your bloody hip flask.
DOUG:	That was just it, old boy. No hip flask.
LARRY:	No?
DOUG:	No. Fell out of me pocket, dammit. Gorn straight to the bottom. Tragic.
	(Front door opens. ENTER simultaneously, JANE from bathroom and JANEICE from front door. They each walk Centre and stop, staring at each other).
LARRY:	Oh god.
JANEICE:	Jane!
JANE:	Janeice!?
DOUG:	Didn't even have a bottle of rum in the bilge hole. Hello, Janeice.
JANEICE:	*(To JANE)* What are you doing here?
LARRY:	Oh shit.
JANEICE:	*(To LARRY)* You told me to come.
JANE:	So, Janeice, I notice that you've got a key to Larry's new apartment. What a clever little locksmith you must have Larry, to spirit your spare key all the way over to Vaucluse. So quickly too. When did you move in here? This morning, was it? Or wasn't it?
JANEICE:	Actually, Jane, I meant to tell you, Larry gave me his key some time ago.
JANE:	Some time ago! My my.
LARRY:	*(Angrily)* Stop it you two. Yes, it's true. I've had the apartment for awhile now.
JANE:	And you just happened to give Janeice your spare key.

LARRY:	She needed it.
DOUG:	Why would Janeice need it!
JANE:	Darling, don't be dumb. Larry's little love nest, of course (*to LARRY*) No wonder Barbie asked you to leave. Did she find out?
LARRY:	I'm not going to discuss it.
DOUG:	Ah, that's what they call a 'No Comment'. Very sensible.
JANEICE:	Well, I'm going to damn well discuss it.
JANE:	About time, darling... (*she sits*).
LARRY:	We can do without your snide comments, Jane.
JANE:	I would have thought that a successful Management Consultant, with a multi-million dollar business, even though it hasn't been sold yet, would know how to keep a party going (*she retrieves her empty glass from where she had left it and waves it at LARRY, who unconsciously takes it, refills and returns it*).
JANEICE:	No doubt you've jumped to your usual conclusion, Jane, which is to think the worst of everybody.
JANE:	Darling! As if I would. How often have I heard you say us girls must stick together. No matter what they (*she gestures towards LARRY and DOUG*) might get up to, which god knows could be anything in my opinion.
JANEICE:	Larry, you obviously haven't told Jane and Doug anything about our agreement... or the reason for it.
JANE:	(*Chortles*) Our agreement! I like that! What about Barbie's agreement? She's obviously the last to know that her husband is an unmitigated cad, and that one of her best friends is a conniving seductress...
LARRY:	(*Shouts*) She suggested it.
JANE:	What?
LARRY:	Barbie.
JANE:	Barbie?

LARRY:	Barbie suggested it.
JANE:	(*Rising*) You mean to try and tell me that Barbie suggested, to you two, that you have an affair, right under our noses, in a ghastly flat that Janeice has had the key of for weeks, with disgusting décor I must say, I must say, Janeice, I thought you had a better sense of interior decoration. How could you agree to it.
LARRY:	Shut up Jane. You want to know what's going on, and I'm about to tell you (*JANE sits*) In fact why don't you all sit down, and hear what I have to say. Here, Janeice, you have this chair.
JANE:	So solicitous, darling.
LARRY:	(*Shouts*) SHUT UP Jane, or you can (*gesticulates*) PUSH OFF.
JANE:	Oh, darling, you sound just like that awful swimming instructor that dear Janeice was involved with...
JANEICE:	(*Has not taken chair*) Jane, it would be helpful if you just concentrated on your drink... of which it seems to me you've had more than enough at the moment.
DOUG:	Damned if I have.
JANEICE:	I know Larry hasn't wanted anyone else to know this, but... Well, it seems that Barbie has a problem. When she and Larry told me about it, I offered to help.
JANE:	Problem?
JANEICE:	(*Ignoring her*) It's a medical problem. I don't need to go into the details. I thought it all through very carefully and I decided to help them with a solution. So we've come to a business arrangement. Barbie did take some time to get used to it, but finally she agreed that Larry and I should try it out.
LARRY:	So that's why I took this flat, a month ago actually, that's why it's all been hush-hush. Up till now.
DOUG:	Makes perfect sense old boy. Anything to keep the women happy.

JANE:	So… who's it to be then … Janeice or Barbie? Barbie or Janeice? Eenie, meenie, minie …
JANEICE:	Jane, you always get the wrong end of the stick.
LARRY:	Barbie can't have children.
DOUG:	Good god! Why not?
LARRY:	It doesn't matter why not, she can't, and it's been a bone of contention for awhile now. And it came to a head when I got the offer to sell my company. What Barbie really wants is a family… you know, kids… more than she wants anything. More than a flat in New York. More than she's ever wanted me, probably.
JANE:	Well at least that part of it makes sense.
LARRY:	Anyway… Janeice came up with the idea, that she could try to have a kid.
JANE:	What!!
LARRY:	None of this artificial insemination stuff.
JANE:	You mean…
LARRY:	And maybe when the money comes through and the kid's arrived, Barbie and I will go away somewhere and… and get used to having it, I suppose.
JANE:	(*Rising*) Oh Janeice! You poor darling, darling. You mean you've been coming over here to get with child. You should have had the place done out, darling, these dried arrangements give absolutely the wrong atmosphere for a fruitful conception darling.
JANEICE:	I suppose you could say these represent … the unsuccessful attempts.
JANE:	Really, darling. How bizarre. I am actually stunned. Douglas, did you say you had found my wrap in the car? (*DOUG reacts to indicate 'no'*) We really must be going. (*Doorbell. All stare at door. LARRY goes towards door*).
LARRY:	What the hell… (*opens door, to reveal JACK and DAPH carrying plastic bags*).

JACK:	Thought you wouldn't mind, Larry, we dropped in on ya with a bit of tucker.
DAPH:	(*Busily hunting for plates behind the bar and beginning to serve up*) We brought it along from our favourite café in Chinatown, lots of chow min, enough for everybody... (*she begins to count up*) let me see, one; two; four; five; oh! (*she stops, looking at JANEICE and realizing that there are six*).
JANEICE:	Don't count me in..
DAPH:	Ooh, Jack'll have to go back and get another chow min.
JANEICE:	No... really...
JACK:	No trouble, love, won't take long...
JANEICE:	Stop. I couldn't eat any of it.
DAPH:	Ooh, are you on a diet, love...
JANEICE:	Not really.
JANE:	Then why all the fuss?
JANEICE:	(*Centre stage*) I'm pregnant! (*there is a pregnant pause... sorry about the pun*).
DOUG:	Er. Well. (*clears throat*) Er... (*raising his glass to LARRY*) Um. Well old boy. Congratulations.
	(*Another pause, perhaps more awkward than before*)
JANE:	(*Suddenly, to JANEICE*) Oh, my god. Darling! Will you be... you know, out in front... for the Black and White Ball this year?
JANEICE:	(*Laughs*) Afraid so... (*gestures big tummy*)... well out in front.
JANE:	Larry, how could you. How utterly thoughtless. If Janeice can't bring a table to the Ball, my party numbers will be right out.
LARRY:	Serves you bloody right.
JANEICE:	Larry... are you going to tell Barbie? Or will I?
LARRY:	Oh. Maybe she doesn't have to know right now ...

JANEICE:	That's not in our agreement, Larry, and you know it.
LARRY:	Well... we could always re-negotiate. What d'you reckon.
	(Slight pause)
DAPH:	Well! Really! I've heard quite enough of this. Come on, Jack.
JACK:	What's up, love?
DAPH:	We're not staying here a moment longer.
DOUG:	You're leaving, Mrs Walker?
DAPH:	Yes. And just as soon as I get home, I'm going straight in next door, to be with poor little Barbie, and to tell her *(looks spitefully at JANEICE)* what her so-called friends are really like. And to think I invited them to our Kylie's twenty-first... *(she pulls JACK by his sleeve to the door... they go, slamming the door after them)*.
DOUG:	*(Going to the telephone, commencing to dial)* Well, old boy. By the sound of that, if I were you I'd get in first... *(hands LARRY the receiver)*.
LARRY:	Well thanks, Doug. *(into phone very hesitantly)*... Barbie? *(pause)* It's me... I... *(speaks up)* Yes I am at the flat... no, I'm not on my own... worst luck... well, Janeice has just dropped in... no, listen, listen, Barbie... you know what you said you wanted more than anything... well... I've got some news for you...

(Freeze frame for about 5 or 6 seconds, then curtain falls).

Frank Sutherland Davidson

BUSH DREAMING

In the Outback, what is real? And what isn't?

Cast: A WOMAN, *brittle urban professional,*
A MAN, *grounded bush dweller,*
THE BROLGA WOMAN, *a spirit.*

Scene I

Setting: *Then, or perhaps now... We are in the Outback, somewhere. There may be bush sounds. A WOMAN comes anxiously on stage. She is lost and disoriented. She carries an old-fashioned walkie talkie that emits intermittent static.*

WOMAN: Hello... Hello... Hello...

MAN: *(ENTERS opposite. Seemingly he doesn't see her).*

WOMAN: *(To walkie-talkie)* Hello. Hello. Hello.

MAN: You won't get a reception here.

WOMAN: *(Relieved to see him but imperious)* Oh! Hello! My car's broken down. I think I might have knocked a hole in the sump.

MAN: It wouldn't surprise me.

WOMAN: The engine just stopped.

MAN: That's what happens.

WOMAN: I'm on my way to Swansville.

MAN: It's that way.

WOMAN: Are you going in that direction?

MAN: No.

WOMAN: I really need help.

MAN: We all need help. That's one of the perks of being human.

WOMAN: Look. I'm really worried.

MAN: There's always something.

WOMAN: If you're not going that way... are you going back that way? Perhaps?

MAN: I live here. I've got my camp over there.

WOMAN: Oh! That's a relief. I can use your radio transmitter. You see... they're expecting me in Swansville.

MAN: If I had one.

WOMAN: I'm due there tonight.

MAN: You won't get there tonight.

WOMAN: If you live here... I'd like some water. I put all mine in the radiator. Of the car. But it wouldn't start. It's a 4-wheel drive actually. I don't know what I'm going to do! Can you help me? Please?

MAN: Come this way.

WOMAN: Where are we going?

(They EXIT).

Scene 2

Lights fade... a faint sound of a didgeridoo. An old woman enters, and crosses the stage dancing... the BROLGA WOMAN.

BROLGA-W: The Bush feeds me. This is my nursery, my pantry and my playground.

(The BROLGA WOMAN EXITS).

Scene 3

The MAN ENTERS, followed by the WOMAN who is limping... she still carries the walkie-talkie).

MAN: I've always found that something turns up when you least expect it. I wouldn't be surprised if that happened today. I've got a feeling about it. There are things out there... you know, forces... that operate. You've only got to look at the way the river floods. There might have been no rain here for years... and then, suddenly, down she comes... running a banker. That's a force of nature... but I mean, there are other forces too, that you can't see. They're all around us... waiting to pounce... taking us by surprise. Oh... if it really happens... you'll know. You'll know if it really happens.

(*Walkie-talkie emits static*).

WOMAN: Hello. Hello. Hello. Oh, why won't the damn thing work?

MAN: It'll never work here (*turns to face her*) It doesn't exist here.

WOMAN: (*Confronting him*) What are you talking about.

MAN: My name's Gavin.

WOMAN: Oh. Does that make a difference?

MAN: The worst thing you can do is to give up hope.

(*The WOMAN stands stock still... they confront one another*).

WOMAN: I thought you were taking me to your camp. Gavin. I thought you had water there. You said you had water.

MAN: There's always water... if you know where to look.

WOMAN: Oh. I suppose it's one of your 'forces' is it. It'll suddenly appear, will it, before I die of thirst. Who are you anyway? What are you doing here?

MAN: I told you. My name's Gavin.

WOMAN: How far is it now? To your camp? I've got to get a message through to Swansville.

(*More walkie-talkie static*).

WOMAN: Hello. Hello. Oh, damn the rotten thing.

MAN: Throw it away.

WOMAN: What? Are you mad? Oh god. You might be mad. Oh god...

MAN: I told you. It won't work here.

WOMAN: They said...

MAN: You've believed the wrong people.

WOMAN: They've sold dozens of these and never had a complaint. They said.

MAN: Could that be because some of the people they sold them to, never came back?

WOMAN: What!

MAN: From the bush...

WOMAN: Oh no!

MAN: This bush.

WOMAN: (*Agitated*) Look. I'm very well known. I do radio, I'm on TV, you might have seen me on the Morning Show...

MAN: We don't get it here.

WOMAN: If anything happens to me this place will be swarming with cops...

MAN: They'll have trouble. Finding you.

WOMAN: Look. Look. I've got nothing you want. I don't understand. I should be terrified... surely you don't want to... (*anguished*) what do you want of me?

MAN: Just your soul.

(The MAN exits... The WOMAN stands dumbstruck for a moment, then runs after him, still limping).

WOMAN: Wait! Don't leave me here! Wait! Wait! Please!

(The WOMAN exits).

Scene 4

The BROLGA WOMAN ENTERS... She walks slowly and purposefully across the stage.

BROLGA-W: This is a place of healing. When the river floods, the old is made new. Lost creatures find new pastures and the fish that live in the desert hatch out of the mud. The weak will find a new strength. This will come to pass.

(The BROLGA WOMAN EXITS).

Scene 5

The WOMAN ENTERS... she has discarded some of her clothing and her limp is more pronounced.

WOMAN: I shouldn't have left the 4-wheel. Maybe someone would have come along the track and found me. Maybe they've come. They've seen the car. Maybe they're looking for me now. Maybe they're trying to get my signal.

(She hauls up the walkie-talkie).

WOMAN: Hello... Hello... Hello... *(pause)* Hello!!! Hello!!! Hello!!!

(There is no answer, not even static).

WOMAN: Dead *(Hurls the walkie-talkie away... She moans and slumps down on one side of the stage, back to audience. Perhaps she could turn round when her speech begins).*

MAN: *(ENTERS from the other side and faces the audience... the following dialogue is spoken in canon).*

MAN: People leave a lot behind when they come here...

WOMAN: I've often wondered how my life will end...

MAN: Sometimes you can watch them as they start to clean out their minds...

WOMAN: I've had nightmares...

MAN: Like when the flood clears out the dry river bed...

WOMAN: A drive-by shooting, breast cancer, suffocation...

MAN: You can watch all the brown swirling water...

WOMAN: I never thought it would come to this ...

MAN: Picking up the dead logs...

WOMAN: Alone in the desert... craving water...

MAN: All the dry stuff that's lying about, off it goes, never to be seen again...

WOMAN: Somehow I don't mind...

MAN: Like so many unnecessary thoughts and attitudes...

WOMAN:	There is a place for me... where it will all end...
MAN:	All flushed away... just like that...
WOMAN:	I just have to keep going... for long enough... to find the place.
MAN:	If you didn't know, you would never think how great a place of renewal the desert can be.

(The MAN EXITS... the WOMAN slumps down as though exhausted & Blackout).

Scene 6

Bare stage... lights up to discover the BROLGA WOMAN dancing... she stops to speak.

BROLGA-W: There has been rain in the ranges... there. Lots of it. The River will flood. The plain here will become a lake of magic. The brown shining water will reflect the copper sun, and fire will be born again on the water.

(The BROLGA WOMAN EXITS & Blackout).

Scene 7

Lights up to show the WOMAN prone as before... the MAN ENTERS. She responds as if in a dream.

MAN:	Here. Water.
WOMAN:	Water.
MAN:	Wet your lips first.
WOMAN:	I...
MAN:	Then take just one sip.
WOMAN:	Oh...
MAN:	*(Not a question)* Have you been dreaming.
WOMAN:	I was in another life...
MAN:	That would be the life you have left now. In another place. Do you really want to go back there.
WOMAN:	It was my life... and it was so empty...
MAN:	You thought it was a full life. You got to cultivate all

	those important people... politicians, celebrities... why, you had all your hundreds of so-called friends... those anonymous people on Facebook you pretended to like. How you loved telling them all about yourself.
WOMAN:	(*Seemingly incredulous*) There was nothing real in it... nothing real.
MAN:	There is a real life here.
WOMAN:	I will die here.
MAN:	To die here... it is the same thing as to live here.
WOMAN:	Is death a dream? Is that it? (*almost a whisper*) Do you have a secret? Is that your secret?
MAN:	Come with me.
WOMAN:	From one dream into another?
MAN:	Under the bright sky everything is the same. This horizon has no limit.
WOMAN:	(*Hesitation*) And yet...
MAN:	If you doubt, you will never enter the true dream. Come.

(He takes her hand & Blackout).

Scene 8

Lights up as the BROLGA WOMAN is discovered C.

BROLGA-W: I have a dream of ships. Of the tall ships that float on the water of the shining sea. The ships are sailing under a sky as bright as a pearl shell. The sun is going down into the evening, into a sunset as red as blood. A sunset as hard as iron. Soon the tall white ships will founder on the iron rocks. Their sailors will be torn to pieces on the red rocks and will drown in the hungry sea. No-one remembers them.

(Blackout).

Scene 9

Lights up to show Man and Woman resting.

WOMAN:	I don't understand what's happening.
MAN:	You came through with me to the other side.
WOMAN:	I don't know what you're talking about. There's no doorway here.
MAN:	There is a kind of door... though you don't see it.
WOMAN:	Everything seems different.
MAN:	You see it with new eyes.
WOMAN:	I feel... free. And I don't know why.
MAN:	This is... a new place for you.
WOMAN:	I am... I am the same person. Aren't I?
MAN:	Only you will have the answer to that.
WOMAN:	Why did I want to go to... to go to Swansville... (*strongly, reverting for a moment to previous consciousness*) Where is Swansville. I must get to...
MAN:	Didn't you know? Once you're here... there's no such place.
WOMAN:	I feel... somehow I feel as though I've been here for a hundred years.
MAN:	Many hundreds.
WOMAN:	What?
MAN:	On this side... time is irrelevant. Just as irrelevant... as Swansville can be on the other side.
WOMAN:	(*Surprised*) I do want to stay here. (*slightly anxious*) What do I have to do to stay?
MAN:	(*Suddenly authoritative*) Admit to yourself that on the other side, you lived a life founded on lies and self-interest. A life that destroyed others, and that will one day destroy you.
WOMAN:	No!
MAN:	Do I have to spell it out? Where are your children? Your husband?
WOMAN:	My husband? I have no husband.

MAN: No. You married him only for what you could take from him. Then you betrayed him. And your children... your living fashion accessories... your children are no longer your children.

WOMAN: How can you say that! I have given them everything... everything.

MAN: Yes. A babysitter and a housekeeper. And the freedom to destroy themselves. Is that what you mean by everything.

WOMAN: I wanted them to be smart and up-there. I wanted them to BE somebody in the world. I wanted them to follow my example.

MAN: Be careful... or you will get that wish.

WOMAN: And why shouldn't I.

MAN: There is no answer to that... unless you can see the answer for yourself.

(Quick blackout).

Scene 10

Lights up to discover the BROLGA WOMAN.

BROLGA-W: This is where they passed... those white men with their camels and their compasses. They could not see the abundance of the desert. They had a slow death, a lingering death. Their lives merged into dreams, their dreams into death. Their dreams were of a sea that they could not find, and so their dreams deserted them. Now even their dreams have passed (*she pauses*).

The desert is always here, with its hidden fruit and its secret waters.

(Lights slowly fade on the BROLGA WOMAN & Blackout).

Scene 11

Lights up to discover the WOMAN sleeping. ENTER the MAN, carrying a petrol can. As the WOMAN wakes, he taps the empty can.

MAN:	You can go now... to your Swansville... if you want to.
WOMAN:	What?
MAN:	(*Tapping again*) So, you see, it wasn't your sump at all. Your car had just run out of petrol. Your fuel gauge is broken.
WOMAN:	(*Social laugh*) I've had such a weird dream.
MAN:	I wouldn't worry about it. Swansville's in that direction.
WOMAN:	You've fixed my car!
MAN:	It wasn't broken. Just... empty.
WOMAN:	(*In a gracious mode*) Of course I'll pay you for the petrol. What did you say your name was?
MAN:	Gavin.
WOMAN:	That's funny. I feel I've met you before. Did you ever work in Radio? TV? The Morning Show?
MAN:	We don't get it here.
WOMAN:	There's something about this place. I feel that I could stay longer.
MAN:	But you want to get to Swansville.
WOMAN:	Oh yes. I have a conference to go to. They're expecting me. I'm the Guest Speaker. I've got it all prepared. "Family Values in the Modern World".
MAN:	(*Amused*) If I were you I'd be in my way then. The river will be coming down soon. We'll be cut off for weeks.
WOMAN:	Maybe... if my schedule will allow it... I might try to come back here.
MAN:	Here, you know, the only reality is the dream.
WOMAN:	(*Puzzled*) I have to go now.
MAN:	Yes. You do. But your soul's desire will return here... often.
WOMAN:	(*Socially*) I'll look forward to it. Goodbye. (*Vaguely, as*

she exits) Oh, and thank you... for whatever it was you did.

(Sound of didgeridoo as lights fade, while the BROLGA WOMAN is seen silhouetted at upstage centre).

MAN: The soul will never be denied. *(shouts after WOMAN)* Yes... come back *(doubtfully)*... if you can... *(he turns and EXITS)*.

(Sound of didgeridoo up... lights fade to Blackout, with the silhouette of the BROLGA WOMAN last to fade).

www.ingramcontent.com/pod-product-compliance
Lightning Source LLC
Chambersburg PA
CBHW021145080526
44588CB00008B/223